MW01182147

"This book is dedicated to the *Cleveland 4* (Brandon Baxter, Connor Stevens, Doug Wright & Joshua 'Skelly' Stafford), and all political prisoners who have paid a price for resisting oblivion in creating better worlds. You are not forgotten."

GTK / PRESS:

Working in the tradition of independent presses since its
inception, GTK Press publishes works of theory, fiction,
poetry, madness, economics, satire, sexuality, science fiction,
activism and confession through several print projects. GTK
Press is a cooperative print workshop interested in melding
high and low forms of cultural expression into a nuanced and
polemical vision of the present.

EMERGENCY HEARTS// MOLOTOV DREAMS

A scott crow READER

SELECTED INTERVIEWS & CONVERSATIONS 2010-2015

GTK PRESS

Dialogues Series
Cleveland, OH

Emergency Hearts, Molotov Dreams: A scott crow Reader

scott crow

2015

This work is licensed under a Creative Commons Attribution-ShareAlike 3.0 Unported License.

ISBN: 978-0-9965460-0-3

Editor: Tom Nomad
Associate Editor: Andy Cameron

Cover: Tony Shephard // www.shephardcreative.com
Interior Design: Ryan Walker
Back Cover Photo: Leon Alesi

10 9 8 7 6 5 4 3 2 1

GUIDE TO KULCHUR
1386 West 65ᵗʰ Street
Cleveland, OH 44102
guidetokulchur.com

For press review copies: Info@guidetokulchur.com

Printed in the USA on recycled paper, by the Guide to Kulchur Print Cooperative Workshop

Contents:

Methods and Proposals

GLOSSARY:

For quick reference in the context of this book, I want to point out words I use throughout to explain social, political, economic or cultural systems.

CIVIL SOCIETY is a term I adopted from *Zapatismo*. I use it here to refer to individuals, organizations, and even small scale institutions as opposed to the state apparatus or even the multinational corporations that use force to reinforce their power and influence. Civil society is you and I and everyone else who associates without coercion.

EMERGENCY HEARTS are these beautiful powers inside us that drive us to action and change in the face of repression and against all odds. The emergency heart is the feeling of empathy and compassion that motivates us to act now to end oppression and destruction. An emergency heart gets people into the streets to resist injustice and create something better. It should never be underestimated in our quest for social justice.

LEADERSHIP (for lack of a better term) represents for me guidance by individuals or groups within communities. This guidance is based in the recognition that there are power relations even within horizontal organizing, based on social, cultural, experiential, or political factors. Individuals or groups in guidance roles may have more power (or be perceived to have more power). The practice of leadership seeks to subvert the familiar figure of the authoritarian leader who delegates tasks, makes unilateral decisions, and takes actions without discussion or accountability to those involved. The practice of leadership seeks to create and reinforce power-sharing rather than power over others.

MARGINALIZED OR NEGLECTED COMMUNITIES:

I use these terms instead of, or sometimes interchangeably with, typical sociopolitical language (like working-class, queer, poor, etc.) that have been used to qualify people or communities pushed to the margins in civil society. Traditional political language takes many of the complex relationships within civil society that make up people and communities, making them one-dimensional. This leaves out the complex humanity of those involved. People and communities are often marginalized for more than one reason. These phrases address the fact that there are multiple issues at stake, instead of running a laundry list to illustrate the marginalization or neglect.

POWER:

I use the term "power" in three ways:

1. **power (with a little 'p'):** power that is exercised directly by individuals and communities, as part of civil society. This kind of power is derived from recognizing that we do have the abilities, creativity, and strength through localized grass-roots engagements to make the world better for ourselves and those around us. It is the collective power of everyone, from the middle class to the marginalized to determine our futures.

2. **Power (with a capital 'P'):** Are concentrations of authority and privilege in economic, political, social or cultural institutions that exercise undue influence on the world. In this sense, Power is by the state, multinational corporations, or the rich, who are not accountable to civil society. Power operates through bureaucracies, executive boards, the military, and transnational corporations and old media. It is exercised through brute force, neglect, and manipulation or corruption of economies, for example. Power marginalizes and exploits humans, non-human animals and the environment treating us all as resources to benefit from. Power actively works to

control resources as well as social and cultural norms. The 1% is another description that describes Power that came out of the Occupy movements

3. I sometimes use the phrase **those who assume to have Power.** It is my way of recognizing that such forms of Power do not have legitimate claims of authority over civil society. It is also a reminder not to automatically give legitimacy to those institutions or people who don't deserve it. My underlying philosophy is that once we see past this illegitimacy, we begin to recognize that we have the collective capacities to directly make changes and influence the world ourselves rather than appealing to these coercive hierarchies and bureaucracies that claim this Power over us.

PREFACE:

The preface used to be a literary form that entailed a certain sort of artistry, an artistry that has largely left the form itself. As the writing of the preface has increasingly degraded into a marketing exercise, one that is mostly constructed in order to either build the image of legitimacy for a text, or to allow some new writer their "big break", we have lost the over-riding purpose of the form itself. What makes the preface so unique as a form is not just that it often tends to be written by more or less prominent people, or people writing prefaces for prominent people. Rather, in the structure of the literary text itself, within the closed universe that is the book, enclosed between two barriers, the preface takes on a role of being both internal and external to the text. On the one hand the preface exists as a space that is intimately connected to the text, and cannot exist outside of the text itself. The text gives the preface a raison d'être, a reason for being, that, without its insertion before the body of the text, it would seem disjointed and useless. But, on the other hand, the preface exists as a space outside of the main body, almost as a conscience or a voice that exists outside of the text, as a rumination on the text, or at least this is how the form was structured before the contemporary period.

In this not too far gone past the preface existed either as a text written by the author themselves, as in the prefaces that Marx wrote to *Capital*, or that Hegel wrote to the *Phenomenology of Spirit*, or by some outsider that felt a unique attachment to the text, or had some intimate connection with its discovery and release. In the author written preface the purpose of the text usually centers around the attempt to respond to some sort of question caused by the original body of the text, and often existed as a sort of response to criticism or discussion of the strategic purpose of a text, almost always written for the second or third release of a text that had already been widely read to a degree. We can also see a glimpse into another structure of the preface, if we take a look at a text like Sartre's Preface to Fanon's *Wretched of the Earth*, which was both laudatory and critical, but spent the majority of the text explaining the relevance of the text not only to contemporary thinking around armed struggle and anti-colonialism, but specifically to the events that were destabilizing the remaining elements of the French Empire at the time. In these examples a common thread comes together, that the preface exists not as another form of introduction, as some sort of entrance into the text itself, or as some way to boost reader interest, as it largely exists today. Rather, the preface exists as a site in which the text can have another voice, one that is connected to the text, but one that also exists outside of the text, a voice that is either a voice of the author in the future, a future after the original text was written, or a voice from another. But, in both of these possible forms the preface exists as a form that exists purely to shift a perspective, to discuss a purpose, to engage with a text and to bring the text outside of itself, outside of the all to often confined and self-referential world of the literary work.

It is in this sense that I am undertaking the writing of the preface for this text, a text which in itself has an interesting temporality to it. This temporality is composed of a specific orientation that this text, both in structure and content, has to the wider anarchist milieu, and discourse in general, and this temporal convergence occurs on a series of levels. The first of these levels is the text itself, the structure of the reader, which in this case is largely composed on interviews. In the interview form there is an immediacy to the articulation, a sense in which the articulation is deeply embedded in the time and space of its occurrence, The text exists not as a singular piece, or even as a linear text constructed of thematically consistent but independent texts, but rather, a sort of movement through time. In this sense it is a sort of journey through a time of turmoil, a time in which many were beginning to understand how to fight, a time in which the dream of Clintonian America, the glass and steel idealism of globalization that typified much of the late 1990s and early 2000s, collapsed into disarray, a time of increasing social and political tension. But, rather than attempting to organize itself around an artificial chronology, something that would be impossible to do in any sort of comprehensive way, this text works through these points of impasse and convergence in time thematically, organizing momentary ruminations in such a way as to build a mutually supporting narrative based in navigating the complexities of this period.

Secondly, this temporality occurs around a series of defining moments for radical struggle within the US. The interviews that form the body of this text occur over a period of time that is interesting for many reasons, both due to the work of the author himself, but also due to the wider experiences that many within the anarchist and wider radical milieu were beginning to come to terms with. From the work around Hurricane Katrina, and the real birth of the idea of an anarchist relief effort, to the rise of the urban riot tactic and the concurrent rise of insurrectionism, to Occupy, its collapse and the resulting impasse that we are currently attempting to work through, all it seems that can often be said is that a lot has happened over the past 10 years. This sort of response is often a response brought on by a sort of disorientation, one that is the result of a space that is at one hand nothing like it was before, while at the same time exists in a way that still contains many of the same problems that it seems as if many of us have been pushing against for some time. Within this space it seems as if a series of things have become clear, and this has caused some very fundamental questions to be asked. Primary among these revelations has been the rising recognition of the failure of activism as a form. By activism, what is meant, usually, is a self-contained political community that presents itself as a privileged site of political struggle, often accompanied by a certain arrogance around political conclusions and a deep attachment to political identity and some moral imperative to act. In embracing this form many problems arose, not the least of which is how purity narratives foster a sort of cannibalistic social scene.

The third temporal plane exists on the level of the temporality of discourse and its disjunction from the temporality of action itself. These thematics are subtle, but play themselves out in the discussions on questions of morality, veganism and what scott is calling pragmatism, or the divergence between these notions of political purism and the functionalities of material activity. All of our approaches to action are mired in this approach which seems to assume that we act as some sort of political unity, and that it is these sorts of political unities that generate some inertia toward revolution, insurrection, whatever we want to term it. Within this sort of closed loop of a universe what is missed is that all action occurs somewhere, in a time, at a place, and occurs within some sort of terrain of material actions. To fail to take this into account, to fail to recognize this, is what has led to the current impasses that we are facing, impasses in which the question is not centered on how we understand the space that we find ourselves in, or the ways that we can gain strategic advantage within these spaces, but remains firmly focused on some sort of conceptual panacea, the right concept, the right narrative.

What I appreciate about this text exists firmly embedded in this series of problems, and the ways in which this text attempts to work through these sorts of issues. In some senses the text is based in a discussion of the meta-conceptual discussion of why it is that a specific person, through a specific series of experiences has chosen a specific side and form of engagement within social war, a question that we all need to answer in our own ways. But, and this is the important aspect of the text, this question is a question that is always firmly positioned within the realm of the particularity of existence, one that is thought through and explained in an almost anecdotal form that allows for us to think back to how we may have come to a certain place in our own lives, a place in which we decided that, in some way or another, it was time to figure out how to engage back, to strike back, even if in only minor or conceptual ways, and sometimes in not so minor ways. This question is separated, to a degree from another series of question however, the question of what this means for us in relation to practice. We can see this in the discussion of the use of media within the text. The corporate media is often villainized, and rightly so for many reasons, but the tendency seems to take a rejection of the clearly compromised attempt to create an acceptable narrative within modern mass media and just ignore the existence of the media-scape all together in favor of minor independent media projects. While, as scott crow argues here, it is important to develop our own means of communication distribution, this does not mean that we can ignore the fact that the modern mass media comprises an aspect of our terrain, an aspect of the space that we engage within. Though I am sure that some will read this as a call for us to become acceptable, this is not the case. Rather, the important aspect of claims like this are that they make a simple, but important and often forgotten claim; even if we do not like something, even if there is a rejection of something, that does not mean that this thing can be ignored in our calculations of the space that we act within.

What is important about discussions like this are not that they come around to explain some sort of "correct" practice in relation to the reviled thing. Rather, what is being recognized here is that the conceptual framing of space is not enough to understand engagement, that purity is not something that is going to allow us to calculate effective action, and that often the reliance on conceptual analysis removes us from being able to calculate what the effects of actions can be on a longer strategic timeline. We could see problems like this arise in almost every Occupy camp, from pacifists preventing others from dealing with disruptive and potentially sketchy people to the often repeated necessity of filming general assemblies, because of the need for "transparency", Occupy entirely imploded under the weight of its ideas, the ways that these ideas prevented actual material considerations from being taken into account, and how this led to a naïvety that, with a few exceptions, led to a situation in which largely minor police action could displace entire groups of people, often without a fight. Now, there were plenty of other problems with Occupy, but these dynamics demonstrate the central problem well, and it is this central problem that scott crow is attempting to navigate within this text. How is it that we can simultaneously recognize that ideas exist in this sort of conceptual plane that is separate from the very material dynamics of actual resistance, while recognizing that we cannot sacrifice material effectiveness for the sake of conceptual purity?

In many ways this text is a text of the impasse, a text that is attempting to navigate a space that many of us are just beginning to recognize even exists. For a while now there has been a simultaneous recognition that something has gone awry in the inertia that many of us once felt that we had, coming out of confrontations like the Pittsburgh G20, and that there has been a resistance in many circles to recognizing that this decline should be causing some very fundamental ideas to be rethought. Once we are able to embrace both of these problems, that we have lost much of the momentum that drove the events of the late 2000s, and that this means that we should be seriously taking a look at what this means for the ideas that many of us had about resistance and fighting, we enter into this impasse, a space in which everything must be called into question. It is in this space that this text exists, as a form of navigation, the navigation of a person along a path through the morass that the radical milieu has become, and like any path, any navigation that does not attempt to become a map, there is something that we can learn in the journey itself. It is not that at the end of this you are going to feel as if you have any answers, that is not the goal of this text, and that is one of the most compelling aspects of the text itself. Rather, in many ways, this text can allow us to come to terms with some of the aspects of the expectations of the past that need to be challenged, broken apart and looked at from a completely different angle of perception. This is a process that this text is not only a part of the process of, and a rumination on in many ways, but it is also a process that we should all be actively embracing.

Tom Nomad
GTK Press
May 2015

INTRODUCTION:
or How the Jukebox Works Inside
(HINT: Push a Button Anywhere)

"My favorite words are possibilities, opportunities, and curiosity. I think if you are curious, you create opportunities, and then if you open the doors, you create possibilities."

—Mario Testino

"The writer treats words as a painter treats the paint. Abstract painters found the real heroes picture was often the paint. Painters and writers want to be heroes challenging fate in their lives or in their art. So if you want to change fate cut up the words."

—Brion Gysin

Hello friends, comrades, readers, and music lovers,

Someone from the peanut gallery once remarked that I was like an old jukebox player when talking ideas, politics, or life. Just push a button and I can start talking about something in pop terms, but without going on forever. I liked that analogy. Just push the button anywhere. The book you are about to read is like that. Interviewers asked questions then pushed the selected play buttons, and I started talking about different ideas and subjects including my life, anarchy, resistance to capitalism and bad governments, transformation of power, of ourselves, making piles of mistakes, political organizing, and dreaming of collective futures.

When Tom Nomad of Dialogues first approached me for a 'scott crow reader' based on past interviews conducted with me, the first thoughts in my pointed head were "who the hell am I, and why collect my windy ramblings?" I was flattered and deeply humbled by it for sure. But at the same time I flashed on so many other voices—writers, activists and thinkers—who perhaps might have merited it more. I would never say I haven't gotten my 15 minutes—and counting for sure—to share my voice in this world. Sure I have been around the block (often chased by the police) and at the barricades for decades (with many rounds of doing community dishes and child care in between), but as the project developed through the support of working with Tom's, and later Lara Messersmith-Glavin's feedback (who also wrote a beautiful afterword), I started to see that maybe my experiences and voice might have some value in the growing chorus of autonomous and collective liberatory ideas. I heard something about my ramblings being accessible to people; I can neither confirm nor deny this, but I'll take it. I am still always amazed, humbled, and grateful that anyone cares about how I am constructing or deconstructing currents of thoughts and social movement histories or stumbling along in life through anarchist lenses.

WORDS, WORDS EVERYWHERE

I am first and foremost a communicator. I love to dialogue and listen. I am far from a schooled or a principled writer although writing has been something I have engaged in to varying degrees since I first wrote poetry and later song lyrics in my band's beginning in the mid-'80s. I have always valued writing and admired people who do write well. Talking and storytelling on the other hand are something I have been doing pretty well since I was three years old. Stories can spark imagination, dialogues, and exploration for all of us, and they always have for me. I have learned so much about our complex worlds and lives, including hidden or obscured histories and concepts like anarchism and social movements from hearing people tell stories; both theirs and others.

BEDTIME FOR DEMOCRACY: THE 80S FOR A SECOND

When I was becoming politicized in the mid '80s it was largely through music. First through punk rock like Dead Kennedys and UK Subs, then later through industrial bands like Skinny Puppy, Ministry, and Consolidated. In addition to the songs and liner notes I read a lot of interviews with band members in both subcultures—paying attention to their politics. Hearing them express their views more deeply in interviews than the songs was incredibly helpful in sorting out more of the complexities of social and political worlds for an alienated teen growing up in a farm and factory town outside of Dallas, Texas, who had grown up on country music then heavy metal, where deep political ideas were obscured or non-existent mostly—except Iron Maiden! Later I read a lot of interviews with people like Noam Chomsky, whose dense writing was often hard for me to decipher, but in interview form I could digest the information. Interviews were a form that made the words more accessible. I still read a lot of interviews today from people who will talk about anything of substance beyond TMZ 'celebrity'.

POST MOD MIX TAPE

Within these pages is more than just straight interviews though. It's more like a literary mix tape—with a weak nod to Gysin's and Burroughs's text cut ups. Some of them have been remixed from the original where I have taken the liberty to expound more deeply on some of the themes and ideas than the initial conversations, cut redundancies or rearrange the order of the questions to make them more engaging to the reader. I view words as living and dynamic symbols to be rearranged, and re-interpreted. I don't want to be limited by the static of print or the rush to the next life endeavor simply because its not very 'writerly'. Oh yeah and I hate having to follow arbitrary rules, so a literary mixtape makes me happy.

So what you have in your hands is not a collection of essays, but a collection of interviews I have done on different themes between 2010–2015 in print, radio, online, and TV. The interviews are vehicles for me, a verbal communicator, to express more deeply ideas, thoughts, and my ongoing political development and analysis. Like my buddy rapper Sole says in his song Don't Riot "… I don't cry for broken windows. I cry for broken hearts, broken promises…". These interviews and writings have allowed spaces for me to vent the rage and sadness around us with my emergency heart wide open, while also allowing the promises and dreams to come out through the conversations with the interviewers.

For some, these words will be new and possibly challenging comfort zones, and for others they may be old hat (no offense to old hats—which are often useful), but I will say they are all honest—warts and all.

My wish is that people will find them useful in destroying Power and civilization as we know it while opening spaces for us to re-imagine and create liberatory worlds from our dreams, first inside our hearts and then around ourselves. In all, remember none of us have the answers, but individually and collectively we have experiences and histories worth sharing, stories for our unwritten futures. Take what you want and leave the rest.

Dream the future, Know your history, Organize your people, Fight to win!

So push the button and play on!

From the concrete jungle in Gulf Coast Basin
scott crow
02. 2015

EXPERIENCES
AND
STRUGGLES

BLACK FLAGS AND WINDMILLS:
Autonomy and Liberation After Disaster

By Jonny Gordon-Farleigh
Originally appeared: STIR Magazine; April 2012

Jonny Gordon-Farleigh: At the beginning of your new book _Black Flags and Windmills_ you quote June Jordan's famous saying: "We are the ones we've been waiting for." Do you think that more people are now beginning to look to themselves for social change rather than expecting it to be delivered by political elites, and thus avoiding the classic disappointments that come, as Cornel West recently put it, with the "appointments" of experts and political saviors?

scott crow: Well, I don't think it is the first time ever but I think it is the first time in a long while. I hate to say this because I don't like to go back to it, but it is probably the first time since the '60s–'70s where people feel that the policies have failed for long enough and that it effects them. There were huge movements for self determination/community control in the national liberation struggles of the '60s and even the anti-nuke movements of the '70s.

Since the turning of the millennium there was a major uprising in the alternative globalization movement of the late '90s and early 2000s that achieved the first international networked solidarity, but it subsided so quickly due to the events of Sept. 11, 2001 it didn't have time to fully develop. However, I think what is happening today across the globe are natural outgrowths of those movements. I think with the failure of the war on terror, the wars on the poor, the wars around the world, what happened in New Orleans, and the global financial collapse, it all represents failure after failure on behalf of governments which has eroded the last vestiges of credibility that the state or corporations were going to help the common person. I think we have historically had resistance currents that have risen to the surface in crisis—also, there has been 20 years of anarchist organizing and growth in the United States, and globally, there is lots of horizontal organizing going on everywhere.

The thing is, I think people actually believe it again—that we *are* the ones we've been waiting for, and I would add that our history is now. The best things didn't happen in the past. They are happening now as we make them. I think that's a crucial change in people's attitudes. Because I think people still, in the United States, had finite hope in Obama, because [his election] was a historically important thing on one level. I *was* moved by it also, and I don't care about electoral politics at all—but I was moved by the idea of what was happening, even though I have analysis about it. But I think the failures of *business as usual* just continued under his watch, and some things have increased like the invasion of privacy and the war on terror, and that's why the 'movement of movements' has risen up in the Occupy Movements in the United States as well as worldwide.

It's also cyclical where things come and go. Having been in political movements for over 20 years, I have seen things rise and fall. But I've just never seen anything on the scale that we're seeing it now, and that's inspiring.

JGF: One of the most overused images from the recent splurge of post-apocalyptic films—where the state and other large agencies are either incapable or unwilling to help—is the presentation of a helpless community that is unable to provide itself with essential services. Can you tell me in what ways the communities The Common Ground Collective worked with in post-Katrina New Orleans provided an inspiring counterpoint to this vision?

sc: By asking the question first: "What do you need for support? And how can we help you build your own power within a community? Block by block. Neighborhood by neighborhood. Community after community." To say that people were helpless is not true. To say that people didn't have resources would be true, but they had the skills, they had the knowledge, they had analysis about it, they just needed support to make that happen. And so Common Ground in New Orleans, in all its ways, was able to come in very under-the-radar to provide the support. But support with analysis in it: we were trying to provide support to build political power and self determination for these communities, not for our own political power.

The government couldn't see it coming because they were so large and bureaucratic. We had horizontal organizing but we also had networks we could rely on. We could be really efficient and flexible anywhere we went because we didn't have huge hierarchies and overhead of administration. If somebody saw a need in a community, and asked the community if they wanted it, we started the project. Or if we saw a need like health care, we started it. We didn't have to wait for a chain of command.

We just saw an opening where we could move in to these spaces. The original dream was to create these autonomous zones like the Zapatistas did, but we weren't able to do that. But we were able to de-legitimize the state at every turn. It wasn't just governments though. We're also talking about the Red Cross who had fundamental failings themselves, and needed to be held accountable, especially in those first few weeks afterwards. The fact that we wanted to treat people with dignity and respect, and to find them where they were at, is really important. Instead of seeing them as victims, we saw them as people who had gotten knocked off balance and we just picked them up and said, "Hey, let's move on forward together".

JGF: The guiding principle of your efforts was "solidarity not charity." How does a group from the outside make sure it does not become a principled vanguard—however well-intentioned—by thinking it knows what is best for the community it is coming to support?

sc: I'd be lying if I said that we didn't. I think that it's a mixed bag—some things we did in deep solidarity; and some things we did were just charity band-aids. When people were starving, we didn't just say, "Hey, we'll feed you." We also asked, "Why are you hungry? Is it because there is no quality education nearby? Are there no decent jobs nearby?" That's solidarity: To say there is no food in your area, and not only because of the storm, but also because of the long, slow history of disasters that came decades before—of the neglect and abandonment of these communities. And so we said we'll help you to provide your own local food security; we'll provide close access to basic health care; and we'll provide job training. These things are all steps towards alleviating poverty. But does that mean that we did that with every program we did? No. Some were absolute band-aids because the state failed to do what they were "supposed to do." So, there were times when we just provided aid because it was necessary—you have to remember that there were life and death situations in the first few weeks and months and we simply had to do as much as we could do, because if we didn't do it no one else would have.

All of this work met with different challenges, successes and even failures. You have to understand that at everything we undertook, even with the best intentions, we were often our own worst enemies, this in addition to all of the surrounding crisis, combined with the bullying and overt threats from the state.

We started an organization based on horizontal principles that I would argue is the largest anarchist-inspired organization in modern US history. We started with a few people who knew each other but grew so rapidly that we had to learn along the way. The politics that I want to talk about for one second are super important. Even though we were inspired to be anarchist and horizontal in many ways, there was also much traditional organizing that featured hierarchical structures. It was a mash-up of the two because of the tendencies that people came out of, the thoughts people had, and the skill levels we all possessed.

In the United States we have a very reactionary political nature and with very little practice in terms of anarchist practice. Anarchist ideas have only really risen to the surface again in the last 10 to 12 years here—in the late '90s and at the turn of the millennium. Thus, there has not been a lot of experience at practice in long-term organizations and these things were working against us. Sure, we had a lot of failures along the way but we recognized that if we could consciously learn from them we could hopefully prevent other movements from repeating the same failures. There were some challenges that we could not get over because they were so large and because we grew so fast. However, there were many things where we could say, "We're never going to do that again." The point is, I don't want to look through rose-colored lenses, which suggests everything was perfect, but it wasn't awful either. Movements always start to look better in hindsight, through the rear-view mirror as you are leaving them.

JGF: The practice of horizontal decision-making has been given a much higher profile because of the Occupy movement, but as Marianne Maeckelbergh argues in the case of Occupy Wall Street, because of the "far greater disparity in terms of backgrounds, starting assumptions, aims, and discursive styles" of those taking part in the general assemblies, it quickly became very complicated. This description seems to reverberate with your experience of the volunteers that arrived in New Orleans. How did you make sure the organization

maintained these values while also encouraging those who may be unaccustomed to the horizontal decision-making model to continue their involvement?

sc: We did it with mixed success. I think the Occupy Movement is a great comparative example because so many of the people involved are coming from different ideas. One difference to us, though, is that we had a large organization and also a closed collective, whereas Occupy camps have large general assemblies. It also depended from week-to-week, or month-to-month, and even meeting-to-meeting, how well they were facilitated and how well the principles of unity were used within it, and how much experience the participants had before they arrived.

We could have two solid weeks of really good meetings and then have two weeks of really terrible meetings that were atrocious. It was always various tendencies of how to organize and always a tension that went back and forth in the organization, but I would say ultimately, if you asked the 28,000 volunteers that were part of The Common Ground Collective in the first three and half years, that how horizontal it was or how well it functioned depended on when that person came in and when they exited.

Now, as far as your question about allowing voices that don't normally practice horizontal decision-making to take part, we didn't. We had to marginalize them because of the crisis generally and then later because of the size of the organization. You have to understand that when it was full-blown, we would have 5,000 people in any given week within the organization. There could be 200 to 300 people at a meeting, 100 coordinators in the core collective, and 150 projects going on. Some of those acted like affinity groups and some of them functioned very well because there was a lot of practice and trust amongst the participants. Other groups were completely dysfunctional.

One thing we tried to do was create a vessel of common values and common culture. It didn't always work well and the vessel blew apart continually, so we had to put the vessel back together. We also had to revisit these core principles as the volunteers changed and as time moved on. One thing I have taken from that, and it is something that concerns Occupy, is that we have to change the way general assemblies operate. While general assemblies are good to share experiences they are not good as a meeting of common values. We need to break this up into smaller groups and find out what affinities people have with each other. One example, here at Occupy in Austin, Texas, is that some participants still wanted to vote for Ron Paul, some participants only care about student debt, and some participants only care about ending the Fed. While, they may have common values like everyone should have clean air and water, this is not enough to gather around. So, what if these people broke-off into their affinity groups where they really had a voice, and then we could start to work together with spoke-council models to find out how we want to resist the current systems and how we want to create new systems.

It is a continual problem in open groups where we have to reinvent the wheel about doing these things.

JGF: One idea this provokes is the difference between formal democracy and substantive democracy. Marianne Maeckelbergh speaks critically in her most recent piece about Occupy Wall Street, of the starting assumptions that many of the participants held (such as scarcity). So, we are starting from a huge legacy of capitalist logic and bringing it to a formally democratic organization (general assembly). While, the alter-globalization movement has quite rightly focused on the 'how' of decision-making, it has also in some ways de-emphasized the 'what' of those decisions—what we are actually deciding about.

sc: I totally agree. What happens is that people mistake the process for "democracy" and they think that if they execute excellent process and everybody's voice has been heard then it's necessarily democratic. Well, this is just not true. On the other hand, all of this takes practice—in our daily lives we all have bosses, landlords, elected officials and corporations trying to sell us shit or tell us what to do. So, the point is democratic decision-making and participatory democracy takes practice.

I have been to over twenty-two Occupy camps and it is a common theme that depends on the respective community and the level of involvement, interest and time working together they have all had. We ran into that in New Orleans but we also had the crisis, so really we had multiple crises. We sometimes had to force decisions through to make things happen and that was the most horrible experience because it would be undemocratic. Sometimes, though, we were talking about real life and death situations which matter more than everyone's voices. But again, it was difficult in general assemblies to make decisions with people who just walked off the streets having the same value as those who were there day to day for months. Giving weight to all of those voices didn't necessarily make it more horizontal, more functional, or democratic.

JGF: Did you find long-term activists accepted these pressures on the decision-making process?

sc: No. By some ideologues we were called the most un-anarchist organization there ever was! [laughs] If you at the look at my writings at the time, I issued several communiqués to address people's questions and concerns.[1] You talked about assumptions and many anarchists and anti-authoritarians brought huge

1   From 2005–2009 I wrote communiqués from the Gulf Coast Basin with reflections, analysis and updates on the Common Ground Collective that were published on INFOSHOP.org and later collected in *Black Flags and Windmills* (PM Press).

amounts of assumptions about anarchism to Common Ground, and I found that to be as problematic, if not more so, than those who had no experience whatsoever. This was a problem because they would say, "You are not doing this right;" to which I would respond, "How many organizations have you been in and how many situations like this have you experienced?" The answer would be, "Never," and I would say, "Well, how do you know if it's right or not?" And we ended up cutting people off when things like this happened. An example of this is when a group of kids wanted to serve only vegan food. This was a noble and beautiful thing but the people who lived in Algiers weren't vegan and it was their community we were in. So, these kids decided to go on strike against us because they considered us to be authoritarian. I should say, we didn't stop them from serving vegan food but stopped them from serving only vegan food. And they didn't have to be in the kitchen, there were plenty of other projects that needed attention!

JGF: Throughout *Black Flags and Windmills* you refer to the Zapatistas' "living revolution" as a source of inspiration and experience. Your own approach reflects this prefigurative 'everyday' politics. Do you think this "new impatience" for a better today is starting to replace the abstract promises of a better tomorrow?

sc: Absolutely. A couple examples of this are the fact that there are more worker-cooperatives in the world today than ever before; there are more indigenous groups taking back their lands since the creation of the modern nation-state. There are local food and local currency movements. That the banks, corporations, unilateral world governments such as the WTO are all too big to fail but yet fail governments constantly, are all indications of the fact that something is beginning to happen.

The fact that anarchism as a tendency, as an idea, as a philosophy, has gained so much ground in the United States, and I would also argue in Europe, more than it has for a long time, shows that people are hungry and waiting for openings like this happen.

I'm not sure how you've been politically organizing in Europe, but here even when I first started to identify myself as an anarchist in the late '90s, and especially in Texas where I'm from, it was not cool. It was very outsider and very difficult to explain to people and I am talking about people on the Left. Communism and Socialism was very easy to explain but to explain anarchism was really difficult, and to be an anarchist was almost a dirty word. If you look now, it is not like that anymore—there are mainstream articles about it. There are discussions about it and it has even been turned into a commodity at stores. These things show that people want to rely on themselves in cooperation without being consumers or voters. I think is really important and indicates that we are moving towards prefigurative projects.

Does it make all perfect today or tomorrow? No, because we still have reactionary culture and politics (as I mentioned earlier). Until we start to dream bigger futures and start to make strategies to move towards those futures, we will be stuck in a reactionary trap or only building in very small places.

I think one of the things that has happened in our movements is the extension of anarchist ideas, and this is small 'a' anarchism—I am not talking of every tendency of anarchism, where we are not building mass movements but rather movements of movements. This is very much like what we did in the alter-globalization movement but much more clearly now. The Occupy groups around the US (and possibly worldwide) reflect this: they are unified on some aspects but are really a movement of movements. This is a development that we've never had in this country before and now the next step is for us to ask, "What do we want a just and sustainable world to look like?" The point I always make is that while we can always resist capitalism, until we really focus on build better worlds for all of us, we will always be fighting against the things that are chipping away at our lives. If we want people to leave capitalism then we have to create something better and show them. I don't think that worker-cooperatives are the answer but they are step in that direction and I don't have the answers but we have to start asking these questions. Then we can all think about our futures and begin to make them a reality.

JGF: This reminds me of the saying, "You make the path by walking it".

sc: Definitely, I cannot say that enough. The beauty of a movement like the Zapatistas for me is the fact that you don't have to have the answer. You just have to know that there is something better and strive for it—even if it is different than you originally imagined.

JGF: Lastly, during So We Stand's recent Aviation Justice Tour, they said, "A healthy community is a radical thing." As a long time activist, how would you describe a healthy community?

sc: On an individual level it is the ability to take care of yourself and the recognition that revolutionary paths take a long time. It is the maintenance of good relationships with others, access to health care, and healthy food. It is also the recognition that we don't always have to resist. On a community level it would look like small, autonomous communities that are networked together for common good. These communities who have their own food security, their own energy sources, access to fresh water, and the ability for people to organize in ways that they want to because there is not one model that fits all. In other ways it could be the re-wilding of a place and the space for those who want to hunt and gather and live *ferally*, to do so without conflict over the natural world.

Basically, it would be communities built in cooperation—not perfect harmony, but cooperation. The idea that we are raising children on the merit of cooperation not their own merits, that we take care of our elderly people, that we take care of the dirty work, of the trash that we generate, the things we create, and maintain the planet with truly sustainable practices beyond cheap oil. All of these things are small scale and it is really about scaling down everything we think we know about civilization. It also means the hard work of "policing" ourselves, where we know our neighbors and we follow guidelines instead of 'laws' because we want to and it is mutually beneficial and not because something or someone is going to force them upon us.

These are some of my ideas of a just future. It takes all of us to do this. No one is going to lead us out of this. We are going to have to do it ourselves.

//

Jonny Gordon-Farleigh is founder, director and editor of *STIR*, a community, co-operative, and commons-orientated magazine. www.stirtoaction.com

THE UNHEARD STORY OF HURRICANE KATRINA:
Blackwater, White Militias, & Community Empowerment

By Abby Martin
Originally appeared: Media Roots / Breaking the Set
September 2014

Abby Martin: Out of all the chaos and the violence that's emerged in the aftermath of Katrina, there's perhaps nothing more disturbing than what happened in the neighborhood of Algiers Point. Just days after Katrina hit, and law and order began to break down, bands of white militias riding pickup trucks and carrying shotguns began to patrol the streets, using deadly force against blacks when they deemed it necessary.

Members claimed they were carrying out vigilante justice in order to protect the streets from looters. But according to a joint investigation by The Nation and Pro Publica, at least 11 African Americans were shot by whites in Algiers in the days and weeks following Katrina. All the while, NOLA police turned a blind eye to the violence.

Here is what a member of one of the militias said about the experience in September 2005:

Militia Member: *"I never thought, 11 and-a-half months ago, I'd be walking down the streets of New Orleans with two .38s in my pocket and a shotgun over my shoulder. It was great! It was like pheasant season in South Dakota."*

AM: Recently, Cam Edwards, host of the NRA's news show, *(ed. note Aug 22, 2014)*, praised the actions of the militias during Katrina, saying that Algiers residents were *"looking out for each other by walking the streets with firearms."*

This rewriting of history means that to this day, there's been absolutely no justice for the victims of these gangs. While in New Orleans I sat down with two men who took up arms themselves for protection against the militias.

Malik Rahim[1] is a former Black Panther Party member, and scott crow is one of the most notable anarchists in America today. Both men joined up to found Common Ground Collective in the days after Katrina, one of the largest grassroots organizations to provide vital social and medical services to fill the void left by government. Over the first four years of existence, Common Ground did everything from building health clinics to setting up housing for thousands of displaced residents. Serving over 200,000 people, and to this day serves as a model for decentralized disaster response from Indonesia to New York. I started the interview by asking Malik if he was prepared for the aftermath of Katrina.

Malik Rahim: Absolutely nothing in my life prepared me for the aftermath of Katrina. The first two days was normal, and then that Wednesday, you know, when people seen that there was no hope, when they seen that the state and the city and the federal government wasn't planning on doing anything; when the horror stories

1   Malik Rahim was the defense captain of the New Orleans Chapter of the Black Panther Party. He, and others, survived two attacks on their HQ by New Orleans police in 1970. He has been a lifelong activist and organizer focused on issues of prisons, environment, affordable housing, cooperatives and political prisoners both in Oakland, CA and his home of New Orleans. He co-founded numerous organizations including Pilgrimage for Life with Sister Helen Prejean, the International Committee to Free the Angola 3 and the Common Ground Collective.

from the convention center started leaking out, then that's when the whole dynamics shifted. That's when Katrina shifted from being a disaster to a tragedy.

In this area here we had a white militia that took up arms. You had to pass a paper bag test. If you was darker than a paper bag you couldn't come through Algiers Point. They had blocked off all the streets. Firemen stopped being firemen and started being guards and the next minute police was pulling guns on you.

AM: scott, talk about the aftermath of Hurricane Katrina— the first 72 hours. What was that experience like for you, and what did you see?

scott crow: The white militia here was gathering ground. You have to understand: they looked like the Klan without the hats. They were driving around in the back of trucks, drunk, with guns point- ed at black people—not anybody else—drawing guns on them, and shooting people. When I first got here the first thing that we did was covered up this bullet-riddled body over here that you could smell for two blocks. There was another dead body over here that was bullet-riddled also. So, who killed them? Was it the police or was it the militia? At the time we didn't know which, because both of them were out of control. The New Orleans Police have a long history of systemic racism and an out-of-control police system.

Basically when I came, I came to take up arms in a community I was invited into, with other people from this community. Two white guys and three black guys from this community took up arms to defend ourselves, defend the community, against being killed by the militia or the police. They were threatening Malik. They were driving by, pointing their guns at him and saying that they "were going to get you, Mayor." (*ed.note the militia often referred to Malik as the Mayor of Algiers due to his notoriety in the community for his organizing efforts*). They were drawing their guns on unarmed people, and we said, "you're not going to do that."

Then the police drew guns on us constantly. This is something that people in these communities have to go through every day, but this was happening to white people who didn't live here. And the police kept saying that we're going to over throw them. But they weren't doing anything to help people; they wanted to restore law and order. You have to understand—there's people trapped in their attics, on their rooftops. We're not talking about a few hundred people. We're talking tens of thousands of people are going to die, and all they want to do is restore law and order, and they're turning a blind eye to the all white militia in this neighborhood.

So, we started to organize by asking the people in the neighborhood. What can we do? They said: *Can you take the rotted meat out of here? Can you take the dead dogs out of here? Can you stop the militia from coming here? Can we get some medical services?*

From that, this beautiful thing started to emerge. We took this incredibly historic, terrible situation and tried to turn it around. Because a crack in history had opened where Power had lost all its control, and a space opened for the people—from us, from below, to come and actually try to do something.

AM: scott, how do you feel when you hear organizations like the NRA actually praising groups like the Algiers Militia?

sc: It was infuriating! I mean, these guys! I was in an armed stand-off with them, and I was thinking: well, maybe I should have pulled the trigger. And I would have killed these people, and I would have gone to prison, and all these bad things would have happened, but it would have stopped them from killing other people.

When I hear the NRA praising them today at the 9th anniversary, I'm like, what's wrong with you? These men and women were killing people and bragging about it. They were treating them like Malik was saying, as "other," as if anybody was desperate was "other," and treated like less than dogs, and they should be killed.

They called it pheasant season. Shooting black youth—they were like, it's pheasant season. I'm sorry to be so angry about it, but it's infuriating. Both the militia and the police. This is the systemic part of this.

AM: Malik, why do you think the government failed so abysmally to react and provide adequate relief in the aftermath?

MR: We give the government too much credit by saying it failed. Because if you say that you failed us, that means that you tried. They never tried. So you know it from the get-go.

sc: Damn right.

MR: You know that we had a ship to run across this levee here, and it didn't break. Why? Because this levee protected whites. It protected the US naval base that was here. So an ocean freighter could run across this levee and it didn't break. I'm going to tell you something. Long before Hurricane Katrina, New Orleans had already been inundated. Hurricane Despair, Hurricane Poverty, Hurricane Racism, that already inundated this area. So you know, the only thing that Katrina really did is kind of expose it. And because that no one cared is the reason why we're facing the ramifications of it now. Because those 9-year-old kids, and them little 16-year-old kids that was in the convention center that you showed no love and compassion to, is now 16, 18, 20 years old, with a gun, and have no love in their hearts, because there wasn't no trauma counselors. The first high school that was open in the aftermath of Katrina for poor blacks had up to 75 kids in one classroom. It had more guards than teachers.

It's not an accident that Chicago and New Orleans have such high murder rates. Look what we did in both cities. We destroyed all the public housing without giving no economic opportunity to no one. So, who was the equal opportunity employer? The drug dealers. Then we put them in jail where we transform dogs into wolves. Wolves run in packs and they kill in packs.

AM: scott, talk about Common Ground. What type of services did the organization provide, and how many volunteers came through and worked with the group?

sc: At one point we had seven clinics running. We had nine distribution centers. We were working with the First Nations and Vietnamese communities all along the Gulf Coast. There were fishing communities, the Creole communities—all these rural areas where nobody was at, as well as what we were going in New Orleans. The thing is, Common Ground operated as an organization but also as a network. We were also spinning off organizations as we went along. We had mobile clinics going; we had a bicycle repair shop which has been spun off. We started a women's center that still exists today. There was the rebuilding. We did worker cooperatives; there was a number of projects.

Any given week there could be 2,000 people on the ground, from around here and coming from around the country, working on 150 projects or programs at any time between 2005 and 2008. People were willing to do whatever it took to make it happen for people they didn't even know. And then, those people who received services had a leg up, you know, we were just trying to build their self-determination for their community.

I think that's an amazing thing, because disasters reveal more than anything the failures of capitalism and governments.

AM: What lessons can we all learn from Katrina?

MR: The greatest effort of Common Ground wasn't the work that it did, it was who did the work. That you had over 20,000 whites to come down into black communities; communities that's right now still classified as being some of the most dangerous communities in this city. That didn't listen to what the media was portraying. They came down here and they didn't find no thugs, they found God-fearing people. Hard-working people that just by circumstance and condition happened to be poor. That's what they found.

And then at the same time that they were dispelling that myth, among us blacks there was another myth that was being dispelled. That was the myth that all whites was evil; all whites was oppressive. Only thing whites wanted to do to blacks was either oppress them or exploit them.

They came down here and they saw this. It was more than just a relief organization. Common Ground came here and brought hope to an area that had lost hope. It brought justice to an area that has thrived and only lived in injustice. It brought opportunity to a community that had only seen despair.

sc: But I think that Common Ground, in the beginning of the 21st century, was a time that people can now look at and go, "this is what people can do when disasters happen." Now, as climate change becomes more real and disasters happen much more; economic disasters continue to happen—the failures of capitalism—I think that projects like Common Ground, Occupy movements, and Occupy Sandy—become this place that people can look at as a reference point to go like: what can I do in my community? Wait—we can do this together? We don't need the government to do this? Oh, we don't need the corporations to lie to us and we can do that? Those are the legacies that I'm the proudest of.

//

Abby Martin is a visual artist, fiercely opinionated indie journalist, founder of Media Roots, board member of Project Censored and former host of RT's Breaking the Set.

Social Movements and State Repression

By Darwin BondGraham
Originally appeared: *Z Magazine*; December 2010

In September 2010, the U.S. Department of Justice's Office of the Inspector General released its report about FBI surveillance of activists and advocacy organizations between 2001 and 2006. Entitled "A Review of the FBI's Investigations of Certain Domestic Advocacy Groups," the inquiry was prompted by Congressional criticisms and media reports about the Bush administration's far-reaching expansion of existing domestic counter-intelligence operations and the creation of whole new branches of the federal police under Homeland Security in the wake of September 11, 2001.

The DOJ review came at a critical time. Almost two years into the Obama administration, federal and local agencies continue to spy on, profile, and repress dissidents and targeted populations. A rising populist right-wing movement with authoritarian tendencies is gaining power. Thus, expansion of police/state power and a cancellation of further inquiries into domestic human rights violations and political repression is likely.

Darwin BondGraham: Through the Freedom Of Information Act (FOIA), you recently obtained 500 pages of FBI files from 2003–2008. You are also referred to in the recently-released DOJ documents that condemn the FBI for shoddy intelligence gathering. What prompted you to dig into the State's files about your life and politics?

scott crow: Since 2001, I have been a supporter of three former Black Panther political prisoners held in Louisiana and collectively known as the Angola 3. Two of them have been in solitary confinement for over 35 years, the longest of any prisoners in modern US history. In 2006, just before an upcoming appeal hearing for one of them, Herman Wallace, his lawyer Nick Trenticosta was shown FBI documents by a district attorney in Baton Rouge that claimed I was an "animal rights/eco-extremist" and potential "domestic terrorist." Within days, I was immediately removed from Herman's visitor list and on two occasions FBI agents came to my home.

This news was not a great surprise. I had first been visited at my workplace in 1999 for animal rights-related activities in Dallas by an FBI agent from their newly formed domestic terrorism unit. In 2000, undercover New York State police agents, working with the FBI, infiltrated, entrapped, and arrested a group of us to prevent civil disobedience at the Republican National Convention. In the years following this, I was part of several anti-corporate campaigns. Private security agents hired by the companies conducted surveillance, infiltrated our meetings, and, in some cases, physically intimidated us.

After Hurricane Katrina, I co-founded the Common Ground Collective with former Black Panther Malik Rahim. We became one of the largest anarchist-run organizations, with thousands of volunteers providing relief and rebuilding in the Gulf. As a social justice organization, we used direct action and civil disobedience when necessary to aid, support, and defend affected communities, bypassing the often ineffectual official channels. For our political views and our methods, Homeland Security and the New Orleans police surveilled, harassed, and intimidated volunteers during the course of our work.

In 2008, 70 pages of FBI documents were leaked to the Austin anarchist community, documents used to prosecute two people, Brad Crowder and David McKay. They had been charged with making Molotov cocktails at the Republican National Convention (RNC) in Minnesota that year. These documents revealed that since 2006, a close associate, Brandon Darby, was a paid FBI informant and possible provocateur. He had been in and out of the Austin activist community and had played a major part in the Common Ground Collective. Darby named quite a few individuals, describing all kinds of activities unrelated to the RNC or the case against Crowder and McKay. In dealing with the fallout, we formed an ad hoc group to gain FOIA's on a number of individuals and organizations in Austin dating back to 2000. Our goal was to see how extensive the Feds' spying on political dissent might be and to share that information with other communities filing similar requests to see what patterns emerged.

To this date, only some of the documents requested have been released, but through this process I received 500 out of a purported 1,200 pages of documents related to my political activities from 2003–2008. Meanwhile, the DOJ has released their report, which calls into question the FBI's intelligence gathering and targeting of advocacy groups during the Bush administration. Both sets of documents confirmed my suspicions about the depths the Feds have gone to in spying on and targeting domestic political dissent, as well as the unfounded accusations and characterizations of political organizers around the country.

DB: How extensive is the surveillance?

sc: From what I can tell from the FBI documents that have been released in political cases in the last two years (Austin, Iowa, Kansas, and Pittsburgh)—as well as state and federal court documents related to the various "Green Scare" trials—the surveillance has been broad, but not very thorough or accurate. At the broadest level, it appears they are gathering mountains of superficial data noting, for example, people who have been arrested at protests or spokespeople for organizations. To me it seems like having a phone directory with thousands of names, but not having any idea who they are or knowing why the names are in it.

On the next level, there seems to be a much smaller grouping where they actually research people and organizations more thoroughly to explore what they term the "nexus of terrorism." These searches are linked largely to certain immigrant groups, as well as social-political activists—largely anarchist, animal rights, and environmentalist. These are the cases where, in addition to deep spying, infiltration and informants appear. It is worth noting that there have also been a few cases of local law enforcement agencies infiltrating non-violent public peace groups.

Cases where they are digging into specific groups or people, from what we have seen in numerous political cases, seem to be much rarer. That is not to say they aren't happening, but we have seen only a handful of examples over the last few years. The use of paid informants is a linchpin. These informants are basically anyone who agrees to gather and turn over information about someone or about groups of interest to the intelligence agencies or private security firms. Informants are untrained and un-vetted people who are put into positions to gather and report information. Often there is no background check on the informants or they are people who have a vested interest in the outcome of the cases due to reduced jail sentences, money, pending charges being dropped, or ideological axes to grind with the targeted group.

This raises the question: how reliable can the information gathered be? If an informant knows the FBI is targeting a specific person and wants to get a conviction, then what is to stop them from distorting information that reinforces what their handlers want? According to many legal briefs filed in courts across the nation in thousands of cases, there are questions about the reliability of informants' testimonies. They have used dubious paid informants in Green

Scare and in the 2008 RNC political cases. For example, in one of the RNC cases, the informant, Andrew Darst, who helped set up a naïve activist in building Molotov cocktails, had a long rap sheet for a number of violent offenses. While he was an informant, he was even arrested for a felony assault for physically abusing his ex-girlfriend. The first activist case he was involved with ended with the activist receiving 20 years. Darst was also going to testify in trial against some organizers of the RNC protests. After his charges made the news, he was promptly removed and never seen again. But the damage was done, the FBI had gotten a conviction.

Informants have also crossed the lines between just gathering information and inciting property destruction. In the cases of Crowder, McKay, and Eric McDavid, the informants/provocateurs Brandon Darby and "Anna," respectively, not only gathered information on activists they were targeting, they actively planned with them and helped acquire supplies that were later used as evidence against the defendants.

In the history of political spying and repression by the State, from COINTELPRO to today, over 80 percent of the targeted groups and individuals have been politically left leaning. The only thing that has changed is that these agencies have gotten exponentially more funding to gather information since 2001 when the USA PATRIOT Act and a host of other bills swept through Congress. Their mandates are to produce results in order to keep the funding for their agencies. Cash strapped agencies are vying against each other for the money and to receive it they have to make arrests. That, coupled with the technological advancements that make it easier to collect data electronically, has led to unsurpassed information gathering.

DB: The DOJ's recent review of FBI spying concludes that: "The evidence did not indicate that the FBI targeted any of the groups for investigations on the basis of their First Amendment

activities," and that "in most cases, documents in FBI files referencing the advocacy groups did not focus on the content of their First Amendment expressions." The report claims that "FBI documents we reviewed relating to the selected advocacy groups generally did not contain inappropriate characterization of the groups." How does this compare to what you have learned about FBI surveillance and characterization of groups or individuals you have worked with?

sc: It was disheartening to see the conclusion because, in at least some cases, it was clear that the feds had violated First Amendment rights. For example, in the Greenpeace case, I am one of the activists referred to in the documents under the pseudonym "Harris." ExxonMobil played a heavy but invisible hand in the local district attorney's directions with the cases. Thirty-six people were arrested for trespassing, normally a misdemeanor. But, through ExxonMobil's influence, they trumped up the charges to felony rioting, although no rioting occurred. This action consisted largely of people in either full tiger costumes or business suits playfully running around on ExxonMobil's property. In the final settlement, the only way the defendants could have the charges reduced was for Greenpeace to agree to stop campaigning and stop protesting ExxonMobil for five years.

It had a chilling effect in numerous ways. First, it ground the three-year Greenpeace campaign to a halt. Second, all 36 activists were unable to participate in any protests while facing felony charges, which dragged on for years. Third, and what was suspected at the time, all the activists were put on the domestic terrorism watch lists after their indictments. They put a few of us under this so-called "nexus of terrorism," a concept repeatedly referred to in FOIA documents. We didn't know when people were placed on this list. We could do nothing to be taken off of it. Being placed on the watch list affected other parts of people's lives, from local law enforcement harassment to being denied entry into foreign countries.

As far as I know, none of the people named in the documents were interviewed for the DOJ report. I know I wasn't even though the DOJ talked in detail about parts of my life.

In the final analysis, the DOJ treated the FBI with kid gloves. The Justice Department made a few mild recommendations, but nothing that is enforceable. It became another meaningless report in changing the FBI's policies or curbing growing domestic spying on targeted communities.

In my case, they looked for funding and aid I may have been providing to animal rights and eco-extremists (to use their terms). They sought to show I was breaking Interstate laws by moving money or materials across state lines. According to the documents I have received, it seems they couldn't link my case to any "nexus of terrorism." Thus, the FBI was not able to indict me on anything related to their accusations, so they closed the investigation. The caveat is that the documents end in 2008 and don't include any of the other FBI documents related to the RNC cases.

DB: What's been the effect of FBI covert operations on groups you've been involved with?

sc: The report overlooked or didn't look deep enough into the chilling affect that the FBI's overt and covert activities have within social justice communities pushed to the margins. These have resulted in widespread disinformation in various communities, distrust of new people who don't express certain preconceived ideas, as well as fear of excessive legal charges from protests and actions. There are many situations where terrorism or conspiracy charges are used to raise small protest violations to felony status. For example, if someone paints graffiti on a building, in most places it would be a vandalism charge (a misdemeanor). But if it has political connotations, especially if it's related to the animal rights or environmental movements, then people can face up to 25 years for the same acts. There is the 2009 case of four animal rights activists in Santa Cruz, California who face conspiracy terrorism charges for protesting and writing in chalk on the sidewalk.

DB: The Bush administration was very aggressive with respect to spying on and entrapping social justice activists. What do you see with respect to the Obama administration?

sc: Bush/Cheney were the worst leaders the First World has ever seen and there was a high bar to pass. Among the many depredations, civil rights were thrown under the bus, run over repeatedly, then thrown away. Unfortunately, from that pitiful low, under Obama it is only incrementally better. Despite his initial promises to create transparency in the government and restore civil liberties, they have turned out to be just that—words. Obama pushed the renewal of FISA [Foreign Intelligence Surveillance Act], which continues to allow warrant-less foreign and domestic intelligence gathering from phone companies and Internet service providers. And the corporations have turned it into a revenue stream, setting up whole systems to make it easier for government agencies to gather information while companies profit from it. All of this is done with full immunity, according to the latest FISA amendments.

In my case, they were able to set up "pen registers" and "trap and traces" on my phone and Internet without warrants or my knowledge[1]. All they have to do is present to the companies a "reasonable suspicion" of some alleged wrongdoing and the companies roll over. These methods allow them to obtain records of who you call or the IP addresses or URLs of websites that you visit.

---

1   *Pen register* or *Trap and Trace* are electronic devices that records all numbers called from a particular telephone line or internet metadata from a particular IP address of a targeted person or organization.

Under Obama's administration, funding for the domestic police state has increased. Furthermore, his Administration has made it easier to spy on political dissidents. What Bush did illegally or immorally has become commonplace policy and law.

DB: What are the lessons that activists need to take from the attacks against social movements and the ongoing police/state surveillance of political dissent?

sc: Without sounding overly dramatic about all of this, most everything that activists fear about surveillance and government repression has happened to me over the last 11 years. I've been listed on domestic terrorist watch lists, which are issued to all levels of law enforcement. I have been in groups that were infiltrated and informed on by operatives, some of whom crossed the line into provocateurs, trying to get me to participate in inflammatory activities. I have had my house, business, and groups I was in under massive surveillance (physical, electronic, photo), both overtly and covertly by private security and government agencies. I have been questioned and threatened with grand juries, visited at my home and work, followed and chased on foot and in vehicles by private security and the state over the years. I have been hit with police batons, tear gassed, threatened, and nearly shot at. In all of this, I have never formally been charged with a serious crime, much less terrorism, yet they have wasted hundreds of thousands of dollars on people like me under the guise of homeland security.

In the last few years, the State has criminalized movements, turning civil activists into terrorists. When groups like Greenpeace, the Ruckus Society (whom I worked for over the years), and the Catholic Worker movement are appearing on domestic terrorism watch lists along with groups like Al-Qaeda, it becomes worse than a sad joke. I have to ask, does law enforcement believe it? Or does it justify budgets?

It is up to us to turn to the tide, to live in the open with clear social and political convictions. All of their spying and infiltration can't stop us if we don't let it. There are more of us. We are more creative, resourceful, and have resolve based on our convictions, rather than money or power. I still live my life to the fullest I can. I trust people and I don't live in fear or hiding. I would be lying if I said the road hasn't been difficult, but the advantages, the camaraderie, the creative people, and the good work thousands have done outweigh the almost insignificant impediments of fearing Power.

I am not being cavalier in saying I believe that, for those of us with relative privilege, it is our duty to stand up for ourselves, as well as in support of other communities who are under attack in the guise of the war on terror. We must stand in solidarity with at-risk communities from the assault on civil liberties and basic human rights. Immigrants, communities of color, and radical environmental and animal rights advocates deserve it. It affects all of us at some levels. Their surveillance and spying becomes irrelevant as long as we focus on doing what we do best—resisting oppression and creating better worlds inclusive for all.

//

Darwin BondGraham is a sociologist and an investigative journalist.

Brick by Brick

By Grayson Flory
Originally appeared: *Earth First! Journal* Vol. 34 No. 2 -
Beltane; Spring 2014

Beginning in the late nineties the radical environmental and animal liberation movements gained momentum with a new militancy both for above and underground activities that included civil disobedience, monkeywrenching, and direct action across the globe. Forest defense campaigns to stop old growth logging and the building of new roads in wild areas in the Pacific Northwest evolved into deep woods autonomous anarchist 'free states', with elaborate road blockades and tree-sits, in tandem with urban actions to bring a halt to the unsustainable practices and re-wild nature. One of the biggest campaigns was to stop Maxxam/Pacific Lumber, based in Northern California, which was the largest landholder of old growth Redwood trees in the world, from logging the last remaining old growth forests on the planet in a fight that lasted for 20 years. Dirty South Earth First! was a piece in that fight.

During this time animal rights campaigns were disrupting business-as-usual against industries that profited from animal abuse in many forms. In 2000, a militant campaign crossed the pond from England with a goal to shut down one of the biggest animal testing labs in the world: Huntingdon Life Sciences. The Stop Huntingdon Animal Cruelty Campaign (SHAC) was a militant, decentralized campaign across the globe that used above and underground tactics to shut down the company and anyone associated doing business with it.

What made these movements powerful and feared by industries and governments was that people involved participated in uncompromising non-violent actions not only at their place of business, but also at the decision makers' homes, to stop profiting from exploitation. These were anti-capitalist and autonomous movements that didn't want kinder, gentler destruction or exploitation, but wanted their targets out of business. Industry and governments fought back by criminalizing civil activists and labeling them terrorists.

For more information on SHAC campaign and a brief history on the Northern California Redwoods campaigns in the '80s–2000s see:

The SHAC Model: A Critical Assessment by CrimeThinc[1]
The Feminization of Earth First! by Judi Bari[2]

Grayson Flory: Could you give us a little history of 'Dirty South Earth First!'? How did it start, how did it go, and what lessons did you learn from your experience?

scott crow: DSEF! grew out of inspiration from the successes of the SHAC campaign, frustrations with the way the Earth First! groups in Northern California were handling the Redwood and Mattole forests campaigns, and our proximity to the decision makers of the MAXXAM corporation based in Texas, who owned Pacific Lumber. They were logging the last redwood trees in the whole world. The tallest, most majestic trees, thousands of years old, were being turned into lumber for shitty suburban houses for a few dollars. Ecosystems that took eons to develop were being stripped and clearcut at rates people in the logging industry had never seen before. MAXXAM and Pacific Lumber had nearly wiped the forests out in twenty years.

---

1   http://www.crimethinc.com/texts/recentfeatures/shac.php
2   http://www.historyisaweapon.com/defcon1/barifemef.html

When Rod Coronado was released from prison for Animal Liberation Front-related activities, he went to the redwoods to work on forest defense, but left due to frustrations with limited tactics and a lack of strategies by the people on the ground. I had been working on the same campaign since 1999, participating in logging road blockades and treesits around the redwoods and doug fir forests, and understood his frustration. Although the blockades and sits were beautiful (and in some cases impressively longstanding), the vibe on the ground was often very hippyish and the opposite of militant. Don't get me wrong—there were committed and amazing people involved, but in the day-to-day it was often young people who were stopping by on their way to some music festival. There wasn't "life is at stake" commitment. I'll admit there's something intoxicating in the beauty of the woods that just makes you... peaceful. I know. It's mesmerizing, even as the law enforcement officers are tearing up your camp or one of your comrades is being extracted violently out of a tree. But I was used to street militancy, and it was needed. The logging campaigns had gone on for a long time, but MAXXAM was clear-cutting faster and faster. The trees were almost gone—literally. Logging continued while people were being arrested and forcibly removed from treesits. Many of us could see that they were going to cut what was left if we didn't change directions.

Around the world, the SHAC campaign had been putting pressure on the executives and associates of Huntingdon Life Sciences (HLS), the largest contract animal testing company in Europe. A few of us were involved in the SHAC campaign in different cities across Texas. Some friends brought Rod Coronado, whom I mentioned earlier to speak in Houston in 2003 for a weekend of action. That's when he and I first met. After his talk we all went around doing a few demos at executives' houses. That's when we hit on the idea that these same strategies and tactics could be used against MAXXAM and Pacific Lumber.

Scott Parkin, three other anarchists organizers from Houston, myself, and Rod Coronado (who stopped participating after the first year) became the key organizers. The ideas quickly developed from there. At first we wanted to name ourselves something serious like Gulf Coast or Texas EF!, like we had done before, but instead the influence of The Simpsons and hip hop prevailed. In one episode of The Simpsons, Lisa joins a group called Dirt First!, and at the time the dirty south rap craze was in full effect, so Dirty South Earth First! aka Dirt First! was born. It was self-mocking and urban-oriented. I wrote most of the early anonymous action communiques under the pseudonym 'whitebread' or 'hooks'.[3] Scott Parkin took the lead on the articles on DSEF! that appeared in the EF!J. That core of people organized the majority of events and actions.

GF: SHAC and DSEF! were similar in many ways. They didn't appeal to corporate or government power, but recognized their own; they were decentralized and they each focused on a single target, rather than a broader issue or bioregion. How did these similar models work differently for animal rights and environmental campaigns?

SC: SHAC was the first campaign I had ever been part of that operated with many explicit anarchist ideals in it. Others I had been in had operated on anarchist ideas in vague ways. SHAC promoted autonomy, direct action, decentralization, affinity groups—and although never explicit, it was anti-capitalist. In its autonomy, it didn't condemn nighttime actions or only promote above-ground actions. Any person or group could research the companies and decision makers who were part of HLS and take whatever non-violent actions they thought were appropriate for the goals. It was also the first campaign I knew of in the US that

3   The name 'hooks' was taken in honor of Herman Wallace, an imprisoned political prisoner who was my friend. It was his childhood nickname because he was bowlegged. Years later I found out through my FBI documents that those aliases had been outed to the FBI by an informant amongst us at the time and were heavily monitored.

was explicit about shutting down a corporation, instead of negotiating for a kinder, gentler version to remain. Which I think is something we should think about again as political movements.

SHAC wasn't about mass political movement-building; in fact, at times it was often decried by other animal rights or leftist groups. SHAC was incredibly successful in a short time for all the reasons stated. Different people and groups focused on more than just HLS directly. Anyone who did business with them—including banking, toilet paper, delivery services, communications, investors, anyone who was profiting from the exploitation—was a fair target. Some of the companies were huge international ones like Bank of America or the NASDAQ stock exchange, while others were small players; but all of them helped HLS stay in business somehow. The SHAC campaign started to dismantle those systems brick by brick. Some companies capitulated after receiving a letter, while others slogged through legal and security battles. It was impossible for HLS to run a business if vendors refused to sell to them, or if delivery companies wouldn't handle the animals, office supplies, or documents, or if a bank refused to hold their money because it was tainted in the public's eyes.

To compare effectiveness of strategies, look at Bank of America as an example. They had kept Big Green (NGOs) and grassroots groups at bay for decades in divestment campaigns. These environmental groups were only asking for crumbs really: slight, modest changes in corporate policy. When SHAC started to focus on BOA to divest completely of HLS stocks, they divested within, I think, two weeks. Activists targeted them all over the country in all of their branches. It wasn't worth it to them, or their toilet paper suppliers [laughs]. HLS finally had to appeal to the Bank of Scotland, a state monopoly, to handle their banking. Otherwise they would have collapsed. No one else would touch them, they were toxic.

Another example was the Stephens corporation based in Little Rock Arkansas, which had invested over $30 million US to keep

HLS afloat. They made media statements that they would never divest or give in to the SHAC campaign. They fought back hard. Stephens hired some of the first security agencies to intimidate and investigate SHAC. One of them was called Global Operations, a real shadowy outfit. They called people involved in the campaign terrorists in the media and took out full page ads making us out to be crazy and insensitive.

There was a week of actions in Little Rock targeting Stephens in 2001. It included home demos, teach-ins, vegan BBQs, and on the last day a demonstration at their offices downtown. The whole city shut down. Bank of America boarded up windows at all of their locations and ATMs. Little Rock brought out their old riot gear from the '60s and called in all personnel. They were terrified of 200 animal rights activists due to the Stephens propaganda. We owned the downtown; we ran through the streets for hours being tear gassed and having rubber bullets and concussion grenades shot at us. I was standing next to Josh Harper, a key organizer, when they targeted him from one foot away, shooting him with point blank in the face with round after round. Then people were finally arrested. A week later Stephens folded. They lost millions overnight.

The SHAC campaign was still in full effect when we started DSEF!. Sometimes we had combo weekends of home demos and teach-ins with folks in both groups participating. Like the SHAC campaign, DSEF! wasn't trying to build a mass movement. We had one goal: For MAXXAM to divest completely of Pacific Lumber and for them to stop all logging. We didn't want less or more unsustainable logging. Daryl Cherney, EPIC (Environmental Protection Information Center) and others had long ago worked out transition plans for Pacific Lumber's withdrawal. The company just needed a reason to enact them. That wasn't our goal, but we respected it. We wanted Pacific Lumber to stop immediately or it was going to cost them a lot of money to stay in business. DSEF! tried to mimic SHAC as far as being an international autonomous broad campaign since there were companies all over the US and Canada that did business with either MAXXAM or Pacific Lumber. It didn't get nearly the traction of SHAC and evolved into a small group of people organizing consistently in Texas. We went after the executives at their offices, homes, golf courses, churches, synagogues, or any public place. Two of them moved out of million dollar homes to even more gated communities, including one of MAXXAM CEO Charles Hurwitz's slimy sons.

We did research on all the shell corporations, officers and ways that Charles Hurwitz and MAXXAM (or MAXXSCAM as we referred to them) hid themselves and their money, including pouring over past lawsuits against them. Then we went after their smaller companies and decision-makers who weren't directly related to Pacific Lumber. There were regular home demos day and night by people we knew and didn't know.

In addition to those battles, there was the incredible blow-back from people within the EF! movement. We were denounced by some California old guard factions as being too violent, reckless, and controversial, although we never physically harmed anyone. Many of the most vocal wanted us to continue with passive resistance and entrenched tactics until the last redwood on the planet was cut. Our approach was much more militant.

Internationally there was a lack of interest. Most EF! groups wanted to focus on their local projects instead of coordinating something larger, which we understood. We weren't being vanguardist, but just pushing the edge of where political action might go. The radical enviro movement had really lost its militancy and was comfortable in the forms of resistance like blockades and treesits. I'm not knocking those, but corporations and the state had adapted to them and expected them. When we stepped in, it was outside the EF! norm. Others had challenged EF! tradition before. Remember the redneck wilderness founders who wouldn't let go of that and considered those that came later just "anarchists?" Something different had to be done, and so we did what we felt was needed.

With our lack of resources DSEF! finally settled into two strategies: home demos and a treesit in a large urban park in Houston near Hurwitz's house. The latter played well with the media, while the former was effective in putting direct pressure on executives. The treesit was started about two years into the project with support from Northcoast EF!ers, who were on the front lines in the redwoods fight. The treesit lasted for a few months, but the home demos continued until the campaign's end.

DSEF! burned brightly and intensely for about three years before going dark. We folded from the combination of lack of wider support and the repression from state and private security entities—including a willing activist who became an FBI informant (one of five in my life!). Publicly MAXXAM wasn't budging, but then shortly after our group ended, Pacific Lumber declared bankruptcy and they relinquished all the land. DSEF! was only partially responsible. Campaign "victories" like these are never clear and always messy "wins." Valuable ecosystems had been saved, but tens of thousands of acres of wild habitats had been lost, leaving small shadows of their original selves.

GF: The summer of 2013 saw an exceptional amount of actions in defense of the wild, including treesits, protests, blockades, lock-downs, property destruction, sabotage and animal liberation. As someone who has had experience with diverse groups and tactics in the movement throughout the years, what are your thoughts on the current state of the radical environmental and animal liberation struggles in the United States?

sc: I absolutely agree. Coming out of the energy of the Occupy camps in the fall of 2011 or so, there has been a crescendo of various political currents building again. It has been inspiring to see reinvigorated radical environmental and animal liberation movements again with a full spectrum of actions all over the place. These two movements had largely become tentative, boxed in, and were at low points. For a brief time in the US there were mostly small actions or campaigns here or there that were engaging, but often isolated and short lived. Many radical tendencies that had been gaining ground were being co-opted or (mis)represented by the Big Greens with their reeking limited liberal reforms or diversion of grassroots energy into electoral politics and market solutions. Both of these tendencies didn't make for much of a fight as climate change careened out of control and the Earth was still being pillaged for "resources" and used as a toxic dumping ground. Thankfully, people have been climbing out of that valley and are being joined by more. We have been seeing a new set of radicalization, new alliances and campaigns, and new energies while breaking out of those boundaries. The pivotal Mountaintop Removal campaigns battled this while also fostering radical grassroots activists in this period, and people like Scott Parkin (of DSEF! and Rising Tide) formed key bridges between the old guard and the new, and between NGOs and grassroots groups.

The question I ask is: why were we having this lull? When taking the political view of rebellion we have to recognize that all political and cultural movements have moments of rupture with great revolutionary potential or intensity followed by periods where priorities and praxis are assessed, lessons are learned, legal fallout is dealt with, wounds are healed, and psychological spaces for longer term projects are created.

The biggest factor to this period roughly 2003–2009 was the expansion in the farce of the "War on Terror" after the passage of the Patriot Act and AETA (Animal Enterprise Terrorism Act) combined with the FBI's prioritizing of radical environmental and animal movements in what has been dubbed the Green Scare. The scope and scale of these wide-reaching investigations, coordinated nationwide raids, grand juries, infiltration, and or-chestrated media smear campaigns was largely unknown for a few years after the turn of the millennium. We just knew the targeting was everywhere; from underground efforts like the Earth Liberation Front and Animal Liberation Front to the grassroots above-ground struggles of the SHAC campaign, Sea Shepherd, Earth First! groups, people like Rod Coronado, Eric McDavid, Marie Mason, myself, and countless others who faced some kind of repression or harassment. Remember too that more "mainstream" radical groups like Green-peace, Ruckus Society, Rainforest Action Network and PETA were also being spied on and infiltrated. For many of us the unknown was paralyzing or disorienting at times.

To lesser degrees there were three other currents that deserve mention as influencing factors. The alternative globalization movements had crested after intense mass actions for a number of years. Also, there was the ending of almost 20-year Earth First! campaigns in Northern California to end old-growth logging in the US which had spawned hundreds of treesits and blockades, but also great weariness and burnout from people involved. Lastly, I think the psychological drain from the wars in Afghanistan and Iraq diverted a lot of focus for many activists from bioregional to larger international issues.

All of these overlapping and disparate currents collided, taking a huge toll on people, organizations, and movements. It was a period of refocusing, healing, legal wrangling, and assessment. It curbed the previous momentum and halted wide-scale actions in the US and Canada. But then the smoke cleared.

Now there is an upswing of broader grassroots energy, campaigns, and groups with new networks and people. The climate crisis itself and worldwide governments' glaring inaction and appeasement of corporate interests to the detriment of ecosystems has been com-pelling people to focus on environmental issues again. It is our lives we're talking about. As I mentioned earlier, I think it should be noted that EF! as an autonomous movement had waned mid-decade, which has happened before in EF! history at the end of long campaigns. Rising Tide North America (and internationally) really held it down during the lull, slowly building a network of autonomous collectives and outposts focused on climate issues and frontline communities being affected by them—like the mountaintop removal campaigns. It wasn't absolutely separate from EF!. In some cases it was the same, like EF! 2.0. And I think the *EF! Journal* did a good job of continuing to disseminate information and continuing the storytelling of these localized issues when the rest of the world wasn't. These pieces really helped provide a springboard for newer anarchists or radical individuals and environmental groups to bounce from once people came out of the Occupy movements. I would even argue that the recent overlapping grassroots environmental movements are more diverse in addressing climate issues, environmental racism, indigenous autonomy and solidarity, as well as the complex issues of globalization, capitalism and civilization as we currently live in them.

//

Grayson Flory is an earth and animal liberation activist from Los Angeles. He currently lives in South Florida, where he works on the *Earth First! Journal*

ON THE
PERSONAL
AND
POLITICAL

COUNTER NARRATIVES:
on Anarchism, Pragmatic Ethics, and Going Beyond Vegan Consumerism

By Vic Mucciarone
Originally aired on Animal Voices Radio; September 2014

Vic Mucciarone: You talk a lot about intersecting struggles and collective liberation in your book *Black Flags and Windmills*, where do you see animals fitting into this?

scott crow: I feel collective liberation ideas are crucial; especially in thinking on our relationships to non-human animals, but also the way that we engage with the whole industrial 'food grid' that includes factory farming and the destruction of the natural world to maintain it. Seeing how our roles as humans interplay on this planet, I think all of those are critical as part of our larger understanding of the world. I think that non-human animals are an important part of that analysis. I cut my organizing teeth trying to stop dolphins from being killed in tuna nets back in the mid-80s and have been engaged in animal liberation issues since. I have always felt that anyone who is marginalized in civil society deserves to have her/his voice added to stop that marginalization. I think including non-human animals are a prime example of that.

VM: You talked about being involved with the animal rights community for a few decades and you say that you have counter-narratives to offer. Could you talk more about what this means for you?

sc: Well, it's analysis and perspective from a history of practice and lifetime of mistakes. It is the difference between theory removed from everyday worlds and actual practical realities. For example, in the '80s and 90s I actually thought that if we could get everybody to become vegan or vegetarian, then we would achieve animal liberation. I wished corporate fast food places would carry vegan food as an alternative, never thinking that capitalism would absorb veganism and just make it another niche food market. It was an undeveloped analysis of the difference between my personal political choice of not eating animals and using animal products and how that translates to larger collective liberation struggles that challenge larger paradigms. There are more non-human animals killed in factory farming now than there was even 20 years ago due to increased consumption and yet there are more vegans worldwide too.

For me, all our realizations, our consciousness, as individuals and social and political movements, come from deep under, like bubbles that come to the surface as they rise up. Where I'm at now is that we cannot have a true intersectionality of stopping exploitation of non-human animals and the natural world until we recognize that all issues are related and that capitalism and its baggage is at the root of all. Capitalism is killing us all across every point. As my consciousness about issues and systems deepened over the decades I realized I don't want a kinder, gentler McDonalds, Burger King— or Google and IBM, for example. I didn't want corporations at all. I wanted something else for all of us that moved us to liberation. Part of my counter narrative is recognizing that the alternative meat products that I wished for, for the longest time are now part of the industrial food grid driven by capitalism. Animals and the planet are still being destroyed.

This analysis, which I had considered for a long time is a counter-narrative in the animal rights sub-culture. I don't want us to be better vegan consumers, I want animal liberation. Which is often conflated within animal rights communities. I think being vegan is important, but it is not *the* answer to liberating animals, but in many circles it gets treated as the main way to stop exploitation. In my counter-narrative being vegan is like voting or recycling. These are steps that you can do that give you access to some power and entry to other tools of liberation, but it doesn't create power and it doesn't stop the suffering and exploitation on the scale we need it to. It doesn't end the systems. Capitalism will treat animals as a commodity until we bring it down.

Obviously, the systems around capitalism are very complex and have the ability to absorb almost anything—even radical ideas. Soy and peanut products are part of industrial farming. As long as industrial farming exists, animals are going to be exploited and we will eat highly processed foods that are killing us. That's all part of a larger landscape of problems with our food industry. I don't want that; I want to think critically about it. Like, what does animal liberation actually look like and how do we get there? Sure it might start with my dietary choices and the fact that I want to alleviate suffering, but what comes after?

VM: You bring up that we need to have more complex approaches to complex issues that have accumulated for a long period of time. I think that makes a lot of sense when you're talking about animal liberation that you bring all the different kinds of components together in order to really bring the changes.

sc: What happens a lot in political organizing and political movements is that we often want a single issue to solve the problem. This is why we must look at multiple points of intersection. That connection of struggles is one of the pieces that led me towards the ideas and the philosophies of anarchy. As political organizers, we can't just look at a single issue and tell ourselves that if we just solve this issue, then everything is going to be OK. Because if the house is on fire, there are multiple points of intersection that we have to work on.

I want to be clear that I didn't make these ideas, I just inherited them from praxis.[laughs] For example, I read *The Sexual Politics of Meat* that Carol Adams wrote in the mid-80s, which drew for me clear connections between what I had thought were two distinct issues—the way we treat non-human animals and women. At that point I thought of feminism as this one issue, and animal liberation as this other. She drew the connections between how both are treated by masculine or patriarchal culture. I found the same with the writings of Marty Kheel, who drew connections between animal liberation and the environment. Both of these writers connected struggles and ideas that at the time seemed disparate. I feel what I am talking about is building on ideas where other people were connecting with larger struggles.

I think back to groups like the Black Panther Party in the '60s and '70s. They had what they called *survival programs pending revolution.* If someone came to them and said I'm hungry, the immediate task was to feed them, but the larger political question was, "Why are they hungry?" Is it because they don't have access to health care? Was it because they don't have access to a good education? Well, let's build some free clinics to get them better health, let's build some free schools so they can get education; the goal being to get decent jobs with dignity and respect and be able to feed and house themselves. Again, they turned a very simple question into this larger connection of issues. So often today in our political movements—especially in the animal liberation movement—until recently there hasn't been thought about connecting broader struggles. It has always been very single-issue, which was important for the growth of the animal liberation movement, but a dead end like all single issues. To think differently is a *culture-shift*; it's time for all US based liberation movements to grow up. When I say 'grow up', I mean in political maturity and analysis of ideas.

VM: Why do you think that grassroots campaigns are so effective to the real issues, when compared to professional non-profits?

sc: There's the whole *non-profit industrial complex*: these giant bureaucratic organizations that often focus on single reform issues that they can win and keep getting funded. They don't go after systemic problems or complex solutions because the funding would dry up. I'm not saying that non-profits haven't done great work, but often they have become part of the problem along the way.

Single campaigns are important in the short term because we have to address the exploitation and oppression that's happening around us, but they're not the answer. Even if we're able to stop suffering in one place it's still happening somewhere else. We need holistic and systemic approaches to it. How do we, as localized and networked communities, take on these local and national issues within single campaigns?

Grassroots groups on the other hand who don't rely on funding from foundations or particular funders are much freer to do what they need to do to make liberation total. I think that's a really important distinction. In fact, I think we need to reevaluate the *non-profit industrial complex*. I call it that, just taking that analysis from this group called INCITE: Women of Color Against Violence, in their book *The Revolution Will Not Be Funded: Beyond The Non-Profit Industrial Complex*. Their whole premise is that marginalized groups, real grassroots groups, people engaged in actual struggles that are controversial or really radical, will never get funding because the large endowments won't do that, as it's too risky for the rich funders. It doesn't fit their criteria. It doesn't have the easy quantifiable metric which funders want.

This was seen in experiences with the Common Ground Collective, an anarchist relief and rebuilding collective I co-founded after Hurricane Katrina in 2005. We weren't trying to get the funding from the non-profit sector. We could see it with the organizations around us that were trying to get the funding from United Way, Goodwill, or Habitat for Humanity. The way that they engaged in struggle was way different than the way we were engaged with the people of New Orleans. We wanted autonomy to work with people and communities in meaningful, power sharing ways and to use direct action—even illegal action if necessary—to do the right thing for the people of New Orleans.

I don't have the answers to these larger questions I have been raising, but think it important to ask different questions and challenge our current assumptions of the way things are and can be.

VM: As an educator, how do you approach the idea of humility, in what we don't know? There is the notion that there's no 1-2-3 step revolution, it's a process. Do you have any reflections about that over your organizing life?

sc: When I was in my 20s, and even my early 30s, I was sure I had all the answers. It was 1-2-3 steps to revolution, and we're done. If we could get McDonalds to have bigger cages for the animals or we get people to stop animal testing—we have won. It is the same with any issue. What I realized is that all the campaigns and plans were all dead ends in the long term. They're necessary, but the system still consolidates power; oppression continues despite all of our political movements' best laid plans. I think all who had the 1-2-3 steps to revolution all failed. I'm not saying that they didn't have good things to happen with them, but they turned into failures. All of the 'successful' revolutions failed. Just look at the Soviet Union, for example. Do you think that's what Marx and Engels envisioned for communism?

Capitalism itself, despite all the planning, is a huge failure for all of us on the planet. I started to actually take in ideas from the

Zapatistas in Chiapas, Mexico; these indigenous people who rose up in 1994 because they had nothing to lose. Five-hundred years of exploitation and death and nobody cared about them. They rose up with arms to defend their communities, to end exploitation on their terms and to build autonomy. They chose not to seize power but to exercise it from below, to have small, open ended revolutions. One of the things that they have brought with them from their tradition was to ask questions. Instead of saying, 'we have the answers and we're going to lead you out of this,' they started by asking different questions, knowing they didn't have the answers to all the problems. This was unheard of in the political circles I had known. Being unsure was seen as a sign of weakness.

In the late '90s, when I solidly identified as an anarchist, Zapatista analysis gave me a framework in which to think, where answers weren't necessary. For me, as a fast-talking white male who grew up in the United States, I think it's really important to be able to say, 'I don't have the answers; I can't lead you out of this'—on multiple levels. One, it opens up the space to show that we're all in this together and must work together to find our direction. Two, it challenges the white-hero myths of patriarchy. Three, I think this is the most important, is that we don't have the answers. No matter what we do, there's always going to be unintended outcomes or consequences that happen. The future unfolds and we cannot know if what we set in motion is going to unfold as intended. I am more comfortable with that uncertainty.

I'm not saying I'm sorry those plans or campaigns happened, they were necessary social and political developments in movements. I just recognize that it didn't create liberation. But I couldn't see that at that point. And the same thing happens today. I recognize that all of our development as political movements will look different in five years. It will look different in 10 years, in 20 years. I don't say this to cop out, or that we don't have any good solutions. We all have ideas and we do put things into action that are important, but it will always look different in the future. What I'd rather us do is ask different questions, and say that we don't have the answers. Start from there and go on these paths together. And as painful as they are, as hard as they can be, or as beautiful as they can be, know that we're in this together and we need to be flexible to change directions anytime.

Let's engage differently as individuals and movements, let's question ourselves. Not to undermine, but to explore. If we hit dead ends, then we move around them, and say 'this is what we learned' and move on. I think that questioning creates a whole different way of thinking about problems. But the non-profit/industrial complex doesn't want that. The foundations don't want that, because they want solid metric answers to things that are way more complex than quantifiable measurements.

I am always about practicality. How do the ideas and questions relate to the brother and sister on the block? I'm from a working-poor family; I want to know how does this relate to my family? I live in a mixed-income community. How does it relate to the people around me? I don't want us to just stay in the theoretical, I want us to figure out how does engagement without knowing the outcomes have practical applications.

Often in 'political movements' we don't want to recognize that we are complex social animals, of many complexities. There are economic, political, social and cultural pieces that are all important aspects of this. Politics doesn't explain everything. We can't reduce everything to a political analysis and make everything go away.

VM: In the face of the complexity that you are speaking about, in which we cease to think in the framework of campaigns and issues, the concept of the immediate victory becomes difficult to quantify. Within complex environments how do we think through "winning," or is that even a relevant concept?

sc: A win is always shrouded in something messier than clear victory. In all of the single-issue campaigns we've ever *won*, I've never felt or thought "that's an absolute clear victory," at least on the level that we wanted it to be. It's always the lowest common denominator, the lowest threshold. It's not compromise—it's attrition. That's always been heartbreaking.

The political movements that are held up, especially in the United States, like the Civil Rights movement, didn't change anything, but it's held up by the Left as this amazing culture shift and social and political victory for oppressed black people. I'm glad it happened, but it didn't change the overall systems of oppression and exploitation—whitey still wins and the wealthy own even more. We still have extreme racism and enormous income gaps in the United States. The Civil Rights movement didn't create liberation, just more integration into what already existed. All the voting rights and civil rights were just band-aids on broken systems. Prisons are filled with people who, despite those civil rights, are treated as second class citizens.

Instead of trying to fight for rights within systems in which we have no control or influence, I want us to start to look at how to build up autonomous power within and without them, until those systems don't exist anymore. At the same time, the systems we are building must also put us in conflict with the state occasionally. We can't just be comfortable and say, "hey, everything's cool for us, we can wait for the state to fall." We must create dynamics that bring us into conflict with Power.

Exploitation and oppression still exist today—we can't have utopia and dream, and not deal with overt oppression on immigrant communities, women, international wars, etc. Repression is happening daily, we have to deal with those issues now. But we can't spend all our time focusing on them while power and wealth continue to consolidate without creating viable alternatives.

VM: You talk about self-determination in people's ability to organize in creating mutual aid societies. How does that relate back to animal issues? In popular discourse humans often take on the role of being the voice of the voiceless, so to speak. It's alarming because how do we begin to discuss the ideas of animal agency without humans having to interfere?

SC: I think part of it is that anytime we claim to speak for somebody else, we need to put ourselves in check. I think that's first and foremost. Like for me, as a male, I can't speak for women; I can't speak for people of color; I can't speak for marginalized people. I can act in solidarity with them. I think that's an important thing to remember, first and foremost.

Non-human animals I view as a little different, if only by degrees, in that I think that there are times when we absolutely have to use our voices for them. When somebody's beating their dog in their front yard, we have to intervene. Of course, if they were beating a person I would probably intervene also. But I think we definitely project on non-human animals many of our characteristics about what they're suffering, their knowledge base, all these things. I'm not saying that they don't have suffering, that they don't have knowledge and caring. I know that non-human animals have the capacity to care and have intelligence. They're not just mindless. But I think that we need to be careful in the way we choose to interpret and interact on their behalf.

For instance I raise female chickens in my backyard. On the outside, you could ask why would you do that if you want animal liberation? My answer is because it's easy, and I would argue non-exploitative. They just run around in my backyard and they drop eggs off. The chickens come from people who bought them and don't want them, so I take them. It's like a little mini-sanctuary. Then I had to ask is it ethical to eat their eggs? I know what these chickens are eating and the chickens are treated well. They own the backyard. It's their yard, they can do whatever they want. I have a shelter for them but I don't lock them up; I don't do anything except take care of them. In some animal rights people's analysis that's captivity and it's just plain wrong no matter what. My argument is that I can't let these domesticated animals be left abandoned; they've been domesticated for thousands of years. I can either just let them go into the wild where they would be killed instantly or I can be their caretaker and receive eggs for it. Who speaks for the chickens? That's a counter narrative in most animal liberation movements. I made an ethical decision to keep chickens in my yard. Moralistically I could fall in line with the animal rights world, and just say, "no, that's wrong." However, I have no ethical problem with it. I can't say that decision works for everybody, but no one can tell me I am wrong either.

So, I think that when you start talking about the ethics of non-human animals, or non-speaking, that it is a really gray area. We need to think about ethics of liberation and not morality. I think the animal rights movement was full of morality, where even having a conversation about these ideas is absolutely *wrong*! There was no gray area. Some anointed movement spoke for the animals. Whereas now, people are asking, what does animal liberation look like based on ethical, personal, and collective choices? Is it always exploitive to have chickens in your backyard? Must you be a level 5 vegan to want liberation? I put myself in the vegetarian category because of that. But that doesn't make me less than somebody who wants total liberation.

The other salient point in your question, is that a lot of times people put the morality onto non-human animals. They're often only talking about urban settings or factory farming. This is something that Karen Coulter, an elder Earth Firster, brought up at the Resistance Ecology conference, which I thought was really necessary for a newer generation to hear. It's a longstanding problem in animal rights movements of focusing only on factory farms and urban setting, but doesn't consider the destruction of the natural world and all the animals killed because of that. I think it came from the moralistic overlay of speaking for the animals and the fact that most people engaged in this struggle are urban.

That's a long process to get to, but I think that when we talk about how we treat animals, people are all over the spectrum. Some eat all the processed food that they want and call themselves vegan, but if the natural world is destroyed to build highways to transport food and to grow agribusiness food etc., we are destroying the natural world, and we're killing animals left and right. Thousands and thousands of animals perish, not just pigs, cows, or chickens; there's no hierarchy of oppression. I think that shifting political movement, in general, away from morality towards a politics of ethics is more important. It needs to be asked, what does that mean for movements? Sure, there are going to be gray areas about what is right, but I think these are steps toward real liberation.

VM: Could you clarify what you mean when you speak of the difference between ethics and morality?

sc: For me, morality is imposed by others, for example, like a group, religion, the state, or civil society which says that our lives should or shouldn't be this way. We have little to no say in how that's shaped. There are some root ideas that I think are important, like rape is always wrong. There's no place where you can make an ethical point that rape is ok, we can all agree with that. We don't need an outside entity to tell us that. We can know it and agree without the moralistic hypocrisy that takes the form of laws from the state or religious piety of the church that often takes the form of social control. We know when things are wrong without being told. Let's take another example like murder. Well, what is murder and is it always wrong? What about self-defense or in retaliation for some other egregious crime? Is there a time when extenuating circumstances make it justified, for example, to stop a rape? This is where ethics comes in. Ethics are moral decisions that I as an individual or we as groups or as communities can develop. There can be gray areas based on many factors. We can have different sets of ethics, which is basically our moral compass, without it being imposed upon us. We come to it because we recognize it's good for the benefit of all of us.

Obviously I offer a shorthand for a much larger and longer conversation, but for me I can't do good while it's on the back of somebody else and I come to that from ethics. If I have to kill and exploit something to make that happen, then that's not good. There's no ethical argument for that.

Some might call this highfalutin' talk, but you have to understand that I'm not a super well-read person and I'm not a philosopher. I am somebody that looks for practicality in life and ideas. I don't say that to diminish what I'm thinking or talking about, but this is just from where I'm coming at these ideas. I would much rather have to deal with politics and a social world built on ethics than on morality. Morality is what's gotten us into trouble whether through the state or organized religion, especially fundamentalist religion. Cultures like that are where morality is externally enforced and everyone suffers except those who made the rules.

I don't know if you ever lived through the Straight Edge movement at all, but that was pretty awful at one point. It was like all of people's ideals were taken to this this illogical extreme morality. I'm OK with people who were Straight Edge. I loved people ethically making their own choices about sobriety and such. But you can't punch somebody because they're smoking a cigarette or drinking a beer because you think it wrong. That becomes morality. How is that different from the religious fundamentalists, or the state that says that something is illegal, even though it doesn't make sense?

VM: You've written before that moralizing about veganism hasn't helped animal struggles, because it's just really collapsed into a subcultural market. Under capitalism you can still have animal exploitation alongside Tofurkey.

sc: This happens and people are blind to it. When I say that, I don't want to be dismissive of people. I think being vegan or vegetarian is an incredible starting point to open your eyes about other exploitation. I think the suffering of non-human animals is the most marginalized, and invisible in so many ways. It's something that's really easy for people to do. It can open spaces where you have empathy for all these other people that you didn't even think about or the destruction of the natural world. The problem comes when it becomes moralistic that if everyone is not a level 5 vegan, then they're not doing anything for the animals. We need more subtlety to be healthy and to move forward, otherwise I question being a part of political movements which want to be morally correct rather than honest.

VM: Why does it make you want to question animal rights movements?

sc: Because we have to ask ourselves, is being a level 5 vegan the most important thing for animal liberation? For some people it's the *only* action they're ever going to take when there is so much more to do. I don't want them to be like the voter police, those who say 'if you don't vote, you have no say'. To them, I say if you vote, I can offer you statistics that show you're wasting your time. If people want to vote, that's fine. I'm never going to vote. But don't moralize to me about it. It's the same thing as being a vegan. I can go through and show you, if you only eat vegan, how you're still actually killing animals every year to maintain that food-grid diet by eating soy and wheat gluten, and other factory foods. I'm not trying to bring vegans down or justify anything else, I'm just trying to set up a critical analysis around it. We need multiple strategies.

I wish we could be kinder and gentler to each other. We're all trapped under these economic, cultural, and social systems. We were born into them. What we're trying to do is mitigate the amount of suffering and damage when we can, at the same time making some structural changes in it.

VM: Talk about anarchy; some background of the ideas, and how they relate to animal rights. Where do you see the ideas connecting?

sc: There's a 180-year history of anarchist ideas coming out of European liberatory thought and thousands of years of similar ideas within indigenous communities before that. Like any philosophy there are many interpretations to anarchism and multiple strands in it that overlap and diverge, but there's some really root ideas that most currents share. Nobody has authority over us: we can choose to make decisions for ourselves, as individuals, and collectively to determine our lives. We're never going to vote our way to freedom. Beyond that, it's open. There's no 'brand anarchy' even though capitalists try to sell it!

Anarchy presents cultural, social, political, and philosophical frameworks for our lives without providing *the* answers. The ideas within it are based primarily on ethical common sense. The idea of mutual aid is that we all work better when we cooperate together. That of autonomy: I am autonomous and create my own liberation, but also strives for collective autonomy and liberation for others. The idea of direct action, that we can take actions without waiting for permission, or the idea of solidarity, that those of us with access to resources whether it's geographic, economic, or physical, whatever it is—that we share those with other communities or other individuals who haven't had access to those resources, to support them in building their power, their liberation, the way they see fit. These are some of the root foundations.

Internationally we're actually in an anarchist renaissance right now. The ideas of anarchy really make sense because they're about power sharing. Nobody has the right to be authoritative over us, unlike the communism that came about in the 20th century where they traded capitalism for another terrible set of social and economic systems. Anarchy really wants *totality* or 'social war' which is the total liberation of all individuals and all communities the way that they see fit without exploitation or concentrations of power. For me, anarchy was the only political philosophy that actually embraced animal liberation and the natural world. Anarchists really think and talk about it. It was one of the things that really helped me see the bigger picture beyond single issues. I was part of grassroots Earth First! campaigns, as well as working in a number of animal rights campaigns and many of them used a lot of anarchist ideas. Small affinity groups, for example, which comes out of anarchist tradition, which is small groups of people working together with no boss. Like all of us working together; no central campaign command telling us what to do, working autonomously.

In the early 2000s there was an animal liberation campaign started called SHAC, Stop Huntington Animal Cruelty Campaign, to shut down what at that time was the third largest vivisection company in the world. The campaign in the US was very anarchist-inspired, anti-capitalist, and militant in that it was decentralized; it used networks, power sharing, and direct action to do what we saw fit to close Huntington and anyone who did business with them. It was single-issue, even as those in it saw it as part of the larger animal rights movement. It wasn't about building popular power or trying to build mass movements or trying to get all of the people in the animal liberation or animal rights or animal advocacy communities together. Basically, the goals were to affect the bottom line and drive them out of business. As part of that campaign, we didn't want a kinder, gentler Huntington Life Sciences. We didn't want Huntington Life Sciences or any animal lab testing company to exist at all. Then, after they were gone, we would go after Number Two followed by Number Three, until there was no vivisection happening. It was pretty powerful because in that campaign, there was nobody directing it. I wasn't central to the campaign at all. I was just somebody working on it with people in Texas. There was no non-profit that was worried about their funders giving money. Basically, nobody was there to say yes or no. It was like, do what you felt that will help stop the company.

Also instead of just going after Huntington Life Sciences, we also went after anybody who did business with them; their banking, the stock exchange, companies who sold them fax or toilet paper. That was a huge evolutionary step in the US animal liberation movement. One could probably argue worldwide, because the SHAC campaign in England, and other European countries has been pretty powerful.

VM: What keeps you inspired to keep striving towards collective liberation, keep educating people about these complex issues?

sc: For me, anarchy opens up the possibility of what the world could look like when we engage differently, beyond how we have known it. A world where we don't treat non-human animals, the natural world, and ourselves as resources to be used, exploited, and extracted. We are sentient beings. We are part of ecosystems, not quantifiable measurements to be plugged into economic systems. What could our lives look like if they didn't revolve around currency, exchange, or profit only?

Sometimes these ideas are abstract, but I don't want to take them so far from our current realities that they are just written words on paper or on an electronic screen. I really want us to ask these questions and begin to really challenge ourselves to say, 'look, the future is open. What's it going to look like' even when we don't have the answers. This is much harder, because we've only been voters or consumers or workers, although many of us have been activists. We are often trapped in thinking those are the only choices we can make. There are all these paths that we haven't even taken yet, which are scarier—but let's take them.

The reality is we all have limited control or we don't have the answers today. It doesn't mean we shouldn't try to correct the ills. There are smart, creative people everywhere. We're all people who are determined to make our lives better. I know that we can create better worlds, so why not do that, starting today, even while some of us are under the golden handcuffs? At some point capitalism will be gone. All empires fall. Is that going to happen next week? I don't know, but I am curious and think it's important to imagine it can be different.

The other piece is that climate change is real and it's going to change the world we know in our lifetime. It has already changed, if you live in outlying, small nation islands, or on the Gulf and other Coastal communities. It's changing our world today and it's going to continue to change our world. I don't want to sound scary, but I'm asking what's the future going to look like? We can either wait for governments to do things, or we begin to take action to change ourselves and the communities around us into worlds which we envision together.

People often say that one is either selfish, or one is giving. Well, what if we're actually both? We can do some things for self-interest, because I think it's in the genetic makeup. But sharing, giving, and cooperating is also in the genetic makeup. If you look at non-human animals, they live in herds, in packs. Solitary animals are much rarer than those that congregate together. We have a bit of both in us, whatever that complexity, whatever that spectrum is. We have a lot of connection. We just happen to live under economic and social systems that reward our selfishness and reinforce it throughout life which makes it hard for us to see. We're like fish in water—we can see the shoreline from below but we don't know what it looks like once we're out of the water.

VM: Do you want to talk about any organizations you are currently involved with, or projects that you are excited to speak about?

sc: In the animal liberation world I love the Bunny Alliance; what they're working on and the ways that they're engaging with an intersectional lens is inspiring to me. Instead of just trying to draw people towards their anti-vivisection campaign, they're actually engaged in other animal liberation, environmental, and indigenous struggles. They're working with other groups and actually sharing their resources to support other campaigns and groups. They're doing these old-school tours right now across the United States which are amazing. Along the way, instead of just saying, hey, we're here to extract from your community, they're also saying, what can we give to your community? They've done projects in support and in solidarity with the Lakota Nation, Earth First! and the Tar Sands resistance. Additionally there's Resistance Ecology, which started putting on these phenomenal, intersectional conferences that we've needed in the United States, which highlighted the connection of struggles and inter-generational struggles

Also within the climate justice movement; the First Nations communities in the US and Canada, the front line communities, and the North American Rising Tide network are all doing amazing resistance and re-imagining of the natural world. All of these campaigns, networks, and organizations that I'm talking about have similar elements in that they're looking for alternatives to capitalist agendas within them. They are all thinking beyond just winning campaigns. They're working on systemic changes and drawing these larger connections.

VM: Any parting words?

sc: I'd like to remind people to not be afraid of the surveillance state or governments. No matter what you hear about increased spying, we'll still do all these things to fight for our liberation, and we have a lot of power. There are more of us, there's a lot of creativity. There's a lot of willingness and determination to do things, and that we can do it. That's not even a rah-rah speech, it's thinking that helps me get out of bed in the morning. I'm honored to be able to share some of my insights. I hope that we all continue to move forward towards collective liberation.

//

Vic Mucciarone works as a community organizer around feminist and food issues and is a cultural producer, currently working in radio.

Anarchy and Personal Transformation

By Baruch Zeichner

Originally appeared: Paradigms Radio; January 2014

Baruch Zeicher: Welcome to Paradigms. I'm really happy to talk with you. It's been years, and you're one of those people who are out there doing interesting stuff. Bring my listeners up to speed on who you are. And then, let's get into what's going on.

scott crow: I'm a father, neighbor, worker, anarchist, a community organizer, speaker, and an author. I'm also a jackass; I can laugh at myself. Those are some labels I'd throw at myself. I've been a political organizer and an activist for about 25 years. I've built a number of worker co-ops and organizations. I've also made a lot of mistakes along the way like all of us who are on revolutionary paths. I'm trying to learn as we go.

BZ: What does that mean at this point in the world now—revolutionary?

sc: It doesn't mean that it's the old Marxist 1-2-3 steps to revolution where everything changes. We need deeper revolutionary change. We cannot reform the current systems. I don't want a kinder, gentler capitalism or a kinder, gentler destruction of the earth. We need revolutionary and liberatory consciousness within ourselves and our social systems to really change these current economic, political and cultural systems. Revolution doesn't have to mean violent overthrow or taking state power to replace it with something else equally terrible. For me, it means building power from below, individually and collectively, and rethinking how we engage in what we call 'politics'. In the past there was 'scientific socialism' and deep Marxist theory that said basically if people followed these blueprints precisely then those at the bottom would rise up and destroy the capitalist state and all would be well, but that didn't happen at all. The Soviet Union, China and most incarnations were failures. Sure country's threw off colonialism and imperialism, and that was a good thing, but they traded one economic system of domination and all its baggage for another one. Things like hierarchies, economic disparities, and cronyism still continued—they just looked different than before.

BZ: Was there a seminal event in your life that flipped the switch and turned this light on, and set you on this path, or was it just sort of how you saw the world growing up?

sc: There's not been any pivotal thing. We're all made of lots of stories, events, and moments, some large and some small, that kind of shape us. I think for me, growing up largely in a rural area, in a largely poor family seeing my dad, my cousins, and uncles go to prison were pretty life-shaping events. Having a strong single mom when it was rarer to see that also impacted me.

Also, I think I was born innately, like all of us, to love the natural world around us. That was something that was even pre-verbal. I didn't want to see people destroy the planet or the people or the non-human animals that were on it.

I can definitely say that I've always created my own path because I didn't work very well going down other traditional ones. For instance I've been terrible at working *for* people—I work great *with* people. And so I've always had to kind of create my own work. I think that being stubborn and hard-headed combined with a questioning mind has definitely led me down these roads. I'm very curious. How do things interrelate? Why? Can we change them or ourselves? Not just interpersonally, but the social, cultural and political systems around me?

BZ: How wonderful that your curiosity has not been quashed!

sc: I'm so full of questions! Even more now than I was, say, even 20 years ago. I have many more questions than I did, because at one point I thought I had all the answers. Right? Then it was 1-2-3 steps to revolution through a political path and we've won. But now I recognize that that's not true. Actually, the more I unfold, there's more questions are to be asked. The more uncertain I am about the future.

BZ: What are some of the questions that you are working with right now?

sc: Mostly ones within a political framework, although I think culture, our environments, and social realities play into it all. Like how do we move from a *politics of opposition*, which we've been largely stuck in in the United States for at least 40 years, to a *politics of possibilities*? Politics of opposition meaning that we are often just reacting to the situations that are around us, like activist firefighters, trying to put out the fires of exploitation that are everywhere without any plans for changing the systems that create them: which has created a reactionary set of politics on the Left removed from civil society and is often insular. Refusal is only the first step. I am proposing that we engage in the politics of possibilities that are non-deterministic; that asks questions of ourselves and others around us that we haven't asked before, and challenges us to really rebuild our political autonomy and our political movements; to rethink ourselves and our communities differently than we have been. That sounds like a lot, there's lots of pieces to it, but these are the questions I've been wrestling with, more so post-Katrina. We're great at rising up to resist, but often the waves crash and dissipate on the shores not leaving much behind to build from.

I think they're important, because we who come out of the Left fundamentally—don't even ask these questions. We just assume that the way we engage in activism or political discourse are the only ways that it should be. What I would really challenge us to ask is if maybe it doesn't have to be these ways. Maybe we need a set of internal movement revolutions that really challenge our assumptions about the way that we engage, and the way we see ourselves.

Let me give you just a couple of quick examples. One is the Zapatistas who rose up in Chiapas, Mexico in 1994. I think that their developing politics of Zapatismo, which borrows from lots of other cultures and traditions, is something that I think we could look to. Not to transplant their ideas here like a franchise, but to begin questions about exploration about what ideas like they have. Why do we engage the way we do? Are there other ways? Anarchism for me is another reference for liberatory ideas that opens the spaces to see ourselves as more than activists, voters, or consumers for example. Anarchy isn't a plan, a political party, set of goals or blueprint, it's just a set of open ended ideas.

BZ: I think you're touching on something that is a critical issue in the development of the human mind, which is moving beyond binary thinking.

sc: It's difficult, especially in the political realm, where we want everything to be binary—it's black, it's white, it's right, it's left, no violence and nonviolence—it's all these reductions of complexity. They're really all spectrums with varying degrees of differences. Where do we want to be on any given spectrum? And how do we get there? For me, thinking this way leads us to ask different questions and present different proposals.

I don't mean to sound abstract when talking about these ideas. But fundamentally I think that first we just have to start to question our current praxis. I've found, from talking all across the United States in the last few years that we don't even think about questioning our structures and organizing. There is no question of "are we stuck in a politics of opposition?" I often hear "this is the way we do things." When I offer that maybe there's other ways that we could engage in 'activism' or our politics, it's met with some amounts of entrenchment or fear of changes within our current frameworks because it uproots who we think we are and what we do.

BZ: When people are seeing things through the lens of either/ or (which is binary), it means they're not actually functioning with their full self in the present moment. It means they're in a reactive state to what's come before, as opposed to being in a proactive state to what their intentions are now.

sc: I would agree, and I think that those false binaries generally play into and support what I am calling the politics of opposition.

BZ: I'm curious if you have any examples from your own life, from your own organizing, of transitioning from that binary place through awareness into something different.

sc: In the early 21st century, right around the turn of the millennium, there had been this anarchist kind of re-appropriation of the organizing concept of *dual power*, which is resisting on one hand, but also creating on the other hand. All our actions should do both. I decided I didn't want to be in any more groups that were just reactionary or only resisted Power, the state etc. I wanted to begin to put into play dual power in our culture, projects and dreams. So for me, the largest enactment was after Hurricane Katrina in 2005, when we started this organization/network called the Common Ground Collective.

From the beginning, we framed our engagements with dual power. We would resist the oppression and exploitation and immediate disaster and negligence of the US government, but we would also work with the people of New Orleans and the Gulf Coast to create the world that they would want to live in, and give them a chance to re-imagine their world. For a lot of people who came, and for myself too, this was a large exploration of that—not just intellectually, but actually physically trying to bring these ideas to life in practice.

BZ: What were some of the things that really worked at Common Ground that created new ways of looking at things?

sc: In the *dual power* framework, many people in Common Ground engaged in civil disobedience to disobey the laws that were unjust and immoral in many senses, but also, were creating or rebuilding long standing basic infrastructure institutions, like community clinics, women's centers, neighborhood assemblies, food security through community garden projects, pieces that would give people autonomy and control of their own neighborhoods and their own towns. These were coordinated and networked efforts.

BZ: In a momentary return to the binary, the so-called Left is often criticized for being more focused on abstractions, and that things don't last. But what I want to point out and name for us, is the kind of projects you just talked about that don't get a lot of exposure in the big media. But there's tons of them out there happening in towns all around the world, of people creating community and owning their creative power to make things better for their neighbors.

SC: I agree they're everywhere. For me, I would call it all anarchy, you know, as a political point of reference, where all these people are doing these things that have similar ideas, similar ideals even, but they look different everywhere and they're not branded as anything. I think that's difficult for us, under these systems, to understand. Not just the political left, but I think largely in Western thinking. Decentralized networks don't have PR firms touting their engagements—they just exist with many different names.

BZ: If we look at humanity as a being that is evolving, learning, and becoming whatever it is, what do you think is happening?

SC: There is a crisis of capitalism and a crisis of civilization as we know it under capitalism. It's more blatant now than in my whole life. Unsustainably using up the earth; soil, water, land, as well as humans, animals, and ecosystems—treating it all as *resources* to be used up and discarded. Conversely, I am also seeing other currents with incredible autonomous local communities taking control of themselves outside false borders worldwide. I would argue it's probably the largest movement like this in 500 years since the formation of empires into nation-states but definitely in all of the 20th century. Communities are breaking away to form localized autonomous regions, like in Brazil with the landless peasants movement; in Argentina with the worker co-op movements and the *Piqueteros* movements, the Zapatistas and farmers in India for example. These people are starting to re-envision their life because capitalism, big-S Socialism and big-C Communism didn't deliver the promises they were supposed to. Instead they ground people up and destroyed their fragile systems leaving them with nothing. So people are starting to take control of their lives again.

The beauty of this is that Power doesn't know what to do with this. They actually don't even understand it to a degree, because these are not armed militant movements necessarily, these are people who are fighting for their survival, largely, or people who are working towards that, or are about to have to fight for their survival due to climate change. And I am very excited about those autonomous possibilities.

I think that with the internet we are able to exchange ideas on a larger scale, so I know what's happening with some farmer in India and it matters to me. I know what's happening to the landless peasant movements in Brazil. Those connections are important towards that decentralization and knowing about them. We're standing on the edge of potential and I'm always excited to see what happens on the other side of it.

BZ: Now, you alluded to something that I think is hugely significant. So the 20ᵗʰ century really saw Capitalism, Communism, and Socialism, as the three main socio-political, economic paradigms. And they've all failed.

sc: All of them.

BZ: There has been nothing created on that megalithic scale to replace them. And what you're talking about is small scale, and it goes back to 'small is beautiful'. That is really what we need in order to survive.

sc: It's what we need to survive, but I also think all of the breaking down and collapse are inevitable. You know, the scaling up of corporations, governments, and economic systems took hundreds of years, then we saw how quickly it failed for the rest of us who weren't in the one percent. All of these current large scale systems are houses of cards that are crumbling. People are moving to localized autonomy out of necessity like India, Mexico, South America, while I think other people are doing it because it seems like a good set of ideas like in the US, Canada, or Europe where the impacts have been as broad or painful.

BZ: I'm sure there are lots of folks listening to this who live lives that are "normal lives"—they go to the store, they go to their job; they have the things they pay for, etc. And yet what I want those folks to know is that what you're talking about, that there is a whole multitude of options that are beneath the surface of what we see as "normal" that are happening, that are viable, that are nourishing people's lives. There's a lot more going on than meets the eye.

sc: I think that one of the challenges of the Left (again, I'm sorry about the political references), we need to talk about these things, or figure out—they're in multi-overlapping social subcultures. For example, there might be a New Age community; there might be an earth-based community; there might be a political community. Even within this there's lots of subcultures, and they're not all talking to each other, but they have similar ideas.

Somehow we need to be able to share this information, not on a central website or a central paper, but somehow we need to share this more and more, so we can learn from each other on how to continue to have best practices. But I think it is happening, though. I think we're in a renaissance right now, because there's more cooperatives than there ever has been in the history of modern civilization. You know, worker cooperatives, consumer cooperatives, agricultural cooperatives, housing. I mean, you just name it; there's more. Not all of them are egalitarian, but there's more than there has ever been. And I think there's more autonomous communities rising up since the formation of nation-states, and I think those are two pretty significant things to think about. Then I think the third piece is the economic piece that we were talking about.

BZ: One of the things I look to is the rise of farmers' markets in the United States, which is really a return to something ancient.

sc: The conservative view would be that we want to look to the past and recreate the past that didn't exist; some mythologized past that they had in the '50s. Whereas what I'm proposing in the politics of possibility, is that we look to the past and we make it contemporary for where we are now. We take the elements that make sense in our post-modern era without trying to return to the 'good old days' which can never happen. The rise of farmers markets and other pieces are beginnings in recreating civil society by creating communities that are autonomously localized but networked, and sustainable from our food security, to health care, housing, child care, community self-defense and how we take care of each other all outside the capitalist, and really any economic systems. These are steps towards those ideals for futures we don't know but are rooted in the pieces of the past.

BZ: I think what drives that looking to the past to recreate it is fear of an uncertain future. Human beings, when they're afraid, instinctually try to find something to cling to, to find a sense of safety and security. We're at a time in the world now where safety and security are mainly illusory. They're not very real.

sc: And I'm one of those people. I definitely want to cling to things sometimes, and feel like a reed in the river. I feel like I'm just getting knocked around, and knocked around more, and I feel like sometimes I do want to cling to a rock. I totally understand that feeling.

BZ: How do you handle it?

sc: I try to be kind to myself and I make sure that I still take chances when I need to. I still have to take the chances like everybody else to make these things happen. You know, like I want to make sure that I don't just get comfortable in certain things. So I'm always looking. Again, it's the curious mind, making sure that I don't have the answers, but making sure that I'm asking different questions; or at least, I'm asking questions.

BZ: How does this ethic of yours show up in your parenting, in your functioning as a neighbor in your neighborhood? What are the practical ways that you see yourself living this?

sc: That I admit that I don't have the answers quite often. As a public person, I try to admit my mistakes publicly. And I don't mean that in a negative way, like self-loathing or self-flagellation, but I think it's part of being real, of being a person.

In my personal relationships, we have good communication. I don't believe that politics is the answer for anything, or the only world-view to look at things in. So, I try to look at it in a lot of different ways.

But in my parenting—you know, my son is 30 now—I've made mistakes along the way. I wish I could have done it differently; I wish I'd been less permissive about things. But I can have conversations with him as an adult about these things. I think that giving myself permission to be a fallible person, you know, years ago when I did that, was really helpful to me.

In my political work, for me, anarchy—which is the framework that I use a lot (again, it's just a political reference)—allows me to have that space, to have that political space. Like, I don't have the answers, but what if we explored these ideas? And then asking other people what they think about things, and learning from them.

You know, that is a good question, and I don't think I have one magic thing in that. But communication, I think, is critical to this. All different forms of communication, but I find myself doing a lot of communicating with people, both listening and speaking. I think that's really critical to all of this, so we can come to a common understanding and common ideals.

BZ: Sounds like you're talking about paying attention.

sc: I often feel like Billy Pilgrim the character from Kurt Vonnegut's novels, where I have one foot in the past, one foot in the future, and one foot in the present. But I try to work to be present. I don't have a spiritual practice for that, but I definitely try to make my relationships healthy; to be in the present as much as possible.

BZ: This concept of being present is something that really came into Western society through Eastern spiritual practice in the '50s, '60s, '70s and '80s. All it means is to actually be in this moment, right now, alive, as opposed to relating only to the past. But just being in this moment—it's really simple.

sc: But sometimes it's not so simple. You know, again, like that reed cast in the water that's kind of getting pushed around sometimes. It's hard to be present when you're like, "I'm just floating, and it's OK."

But when I come back to that, there's always security in that. Even in the unknown, there's much more security, even if I'm not clinging to the rock of stability. Just going, "I'm just floating, and it's OK."

All of these things, I think, have taken a long time to get to. And again, I don't feel like I'm there. I think I'm just trying to be there. Somebody had said to me years ago: "Being present is when you look at a flower, before you start to name it." Not in the name of the flower, but like, say, "oh, that's beautiful," or "that smells good." Being present is when you just first look at it.

And I was like, oh yeah, that makes sense. So I do find myself doing that. You know, trying to not name things; trying not to put value judgments on things. You know, it's always a challenge.

BZ: So the work of creating a new human future really starts with each of us doing that simple thing of paying attention, and being in our encounters.

sc: I think that's the first baby-steps. And I think the other thing is for us to recognize that we are not free in our minds a lot of times. We're not free in our souls. And what does liberation look like? This is not even a political reference, but what does it mean spiritually, what does it mean poetically, what does it mean romantically? What does it mean psychologically to be free? I think there's many, many paths to getting that, but being present is one of those steps in trying to forge these paths.

BZ: And there's these distractions that we fall into called belief or ideology.

sc: For sure. because it is like clinging to that rock. Right? Because it's *the known*. I think it's really hard for people to get away from, especially in the political realm where I'm engaged quite often. I'm sure its in religious or spiritual realms also. It's very common.

BZ: An interesting challenge for each of us would be to notice when we're operating from belief, and when we're really in that moment of encounter, and see how much choice we have about that.

sc: Because what is being free—really—is choice. What we at least perceive as choice. I don't even want to get into subatomic cosmological levels of those things, but for sure (or biological things about choice), but yeah—it's that moment when we realize that we are functioning and free.

It's taking that political frame of seeing the world to the next steps for people. Because I want liberation for everybody, I don't want to just have it for myself. And again, I'm not trying to convert anybody either, but I want to share ideas with people so they can be free on their own terms. Then we can begin to rebuild civil society, and our communities, the way that we want to. And ourselves even, if that's the only step that we're at.

BZ: It's another ancient call. The call to freedom and liberation that's real.

sc: I think we're innately born with that. And you know, our social, economic systems, our political systems, just beat it out of us from a young age, and we need to reclaim it. Reclaim that freedom, reclaim that liberation on our own terms, the best that we can. But again, not just for myself, because I don't want to do better while others are suffering. I also want to alleviate suffering that's around me. I think that's really important to engage in both to the best that we can.

BZ: Is there something that's inspiring you these days?

sc: I find incredible inspirations in the anarchist traditions of not being dogmatic, not being ideological. And again, anarchy is a set of ideas that are older than when some old dead Europeans named them 150 years ago. Also the evolving ideas of Zapatismo in the last 20 years—which I have some critiques of, but overall, the inspiration that I've gotten from seeing them make them real changed my political world. Both of these traditions point to engagements of non-deterministic politics towards politics of possibility. Both of these paths say that we don't have the answer, and we don't want you to follow us, but let's all work on this together where we each live in our own ways. I think that there's just so much power in that because one, it's not theoretical; two, because it's so fallible; and three, these ideas can have a practical application and impact for our everyday lives.

BZ: You had mentioned earlier how often in the Left we talk about ideas that don't have, and aren't rooted in reality or practicality. I think it's true that we often have these intellectual thinkers who don't really see these ideas that don't really fit in with the rest of civil society. So, we end up preaching to the choir in political realms and ignoring everyone else.

sc: I'm a high school dropout. Where I come from ideas and praxis have to make sense to the brother and sister on the block or to someone like my mom. She's a smart and strong woman, but she's not an intellectual, so it has to make sense to her life or its almost useless. I don't think we should have to know a secret coded language to express dissatisfaction with current systems or dreams of better worlds. I often ask how do we make things relevant to people's lives?

BZ: Any parting words?

sc: We can't reform the systems that we have in place. We must have liberatory consciousness about them, and liberatory changes to dismantle and build something other. Even if we don't know what it will be. That's not just rhetoric. We can call it whatever we want to, but it's going to take all of us to do it. Nobody is going to do this by themselves. There's going to be no leader, no program, no party that's going to lead us out of it. We're going to lead ourselves. It's like June Jordan said, "We are the ones we've been waiting for." I challenge us to move towards those possibilities.

//

Baruch Zeichner produces and hosts a radio program called Paradigms. He practiced psychotherapy in Vermont for 25 years, was a first responder in New Orleans in 2005, teaches university classes about climate change. Baruch sees himself as a world citizen, and believes in the possibility of peace.

Anarchist Story-Telling:
Reflections on News Media
as a Site of Struggle

By Matt Tedrow
Originally conducted: January 2015

This is an edited excerpt from a longer interview by Matt Tedrow for his doctoral dissertation, and future book which examines anarchism's relationship to critical media theories.

Matt Tedrow: You mention that you're a little "a" anarchist. How do you think that influences your interactions with media?

scott crow: Because most mainstream news stories make me gag, [laughs] due to their superficiality in the way that they will never actually look at a story in-depth. It's amazing how TV in particular can be on 24/7 and be filled with mindless, repetitive drivel sold as 'breaking news' or updates. And in print it's similar, even though agencies can write pieces as long as they want for the web. They still are stuck in these old corporate models of disseminating news, party politics, and corporate agendas. It's problematic across all the big news outlets like CNN, MSNBC, Fox, the New York Times, or others. Thank goodness for outlets like Democracy Now! or online sources like Al Jazeera, The Guardian, and Vice. In fact, in the US, on RT News (Russia Today)—which is total propaganda for Russia—there's a show called Breaking the Set, which is really working to break out of that old cable news paradigm. Besides radical subcultural online reporting these are the only news organizations or shows that will even attempt in-depth coverage that might reach larger civil society, and they're small compared to the rest. They ask, what else is there out there?

When I look at the media landscape, it's through multiple lenses, but mostly through an anarchist lens—that is, outside the mainstream. A lot of times, when big media are talking about a problem, an issue, or a problem's solutions, it's always within a capitalist or the state's framing without question. Or worse, through simplistic false binaries; the issue has to be either this or that. No gray area, so they wrap it up tightly. The questions are always the same. What's the government going to do about this? How's the corporation going to deal with this? I ask the questions, how do *we* want to solve this problem? Why are they only talking about this part of these issues? Why is this 'story' important at all? Are there other ways than just the predetermined scripted ways to talk about these issues or solutions? Even if we don't have the answers at that moment, the media largely controls the conversations and possibly limits the choices of actions that might be taken since it falls outside of the 'script'.

But then there are other questions I ask, too. Why are the media asking only *these* questions? Why are they looking at it from *this* particular lens? And why are they pretending to be unbiased about it? Or what is it that's omitted from the story?

Another anarchist lens, rooted in anti-oppression or collective liberation foundations, why is it that mostly only older white dudes or white women who look a certain way are always on the screen talking? Even for our conversation today, why are you talking to me? I'm not kicking you. I don't want anybody to feel guilty about it. I don't feel guilty. But so often in media they're not even thinking about it. You're hardly ever going to see a radical black person in a dashiki with New African language speaking on a talk show about an issue like police brutality in communities for example. You're going to see a Jesse Jackson type or worse who has been absorbed into that larger white power structure—that speaks and looks the same as that structure brought in to represent voices that have little or no connection to marginalized communities. And if the media does have somebody who is traditionally marginalized, they're going to tokenize them while dismissing or minimizing their views.

Other anarchist lenses might be to ask questions that are being ignored because they fall outside of the conventional narratives, or how can we bring views that are being left out into conversations in big media? Or better, how can we tell these stories ourselves through channels outside of big media?

And I see *shifting culture*, especially within media, as very powerful tool. Shifting culture is a concept that all radical ideas slowly move from the margins to become accepted and eventually absorbed amongst individuals or civil society. Radical culture shifts in people well before reactionary laws are enacted or corporations figure out how to commodify them. Some brief examples would be being vegan, climate change, or the ideas of anarchy. All of these started out in some marginal places, and seen as crazy or wild, before becoming more accepted, to whatever degrees they are. There were times when you said you were vegan or that climate change was human induced and people would have berated you, but through time these ideas became common place whether people agree on them or not.

MT: You've mentioned historical cases where marginalized ideas made their way into the mainstream. Can you talk about contemporary efforts to spread radical ideas in popular culture?

sc: I think if radicals, anarchists, or activists think about our influences on shifting culture it's another form of creating our own power and narratives. Media is one of the most powerful inoculators and transmitters of culture—so powerful that some anarchist friends of mine, who also see the power of shifting culture through media, started a collaborative anarchist PR (public relations) project called

Agency. I collaborate with them by sitting on the advisory board, and write for them occasionally. The idea behind anarchist 'public relations' is that mainstream civil society is talking about anarchy whether we as anarchists do or not. So, we asked are we going to let big media control the narrative, or do we want to influence and create our own narratives as best we can, recognizing that we will never have complete control over them? Agency doesn't claim to represent all anarchists or all anarchist ideas, but creates a space where anarchists can weigh in on social, cultural, political, and economic topics from anarchist perspectives in corporate and grassroots media.

I've been engaged for the last 15 years in contributing to shaping and influencing the way that anarchism is talked about within media, as well as amongst ourselves in the United States. I have done and do a lot of background speaking to journalists. Connecting them to anarchist people, ideas, and projects and perspectives. I've written books and given workshops. I do interviews when people want to talk about these ideas. I speak at college campuses. I have done all this, not because I'm tooting my own horn, but because these are the ways to shift culture, to get people to think differently about their perceptions and world views—to move ideas from the margins to the mainstream. The results have been mixed, but support for anarchist ideas has grown exponentially across many places due to anarchists actively engaged in the narratives within big media and grassroots media.

MT: Is it even worth doing that sort of thing? 'Anarchy' has always been sort of a bad word in the mouths and minds of many people.

sc: But 'anarchism' is just a word. It's just a point of reference to a larger set of liberatory ideas. I don't give a shit if we call it 'blue potato'. In Latin America, when they didn't want to have the baggage of communism and anarchism, they use 'horizontalism' in Argentina or 'Zapatismo' from the Zapatistas in Mexico. I don't care. But it's a little harder in the United States to invent new words and make them have currency, so the word anarchy remains the shorthand. What I'm interested in is, presenting and stretching those liberatory ideas. And that happens regularly. Anarchists in the US have changed the dialogue in the last 15 years—not just myself, but all of us who have engaged with that media. What I really want is for people to get past the single words, to those ideas, those stories. Can we get those ideas talked about in big media in addition to ourselves?

For me, shifting culture is more than just putting anarchist and radical ideas into mainstream media, but also, and possibly more importantly, about building our own grassroots media, our counter and alternative media—which I don't even look at as alternatives—but really as building new media outside of the traditional Fifth Estate models. To be able to tell our own narratives and stories, our own dreams our way without their filters, bias, and distortions. And that part, I feel, has been incredibly powerful in the last few years as the internet and DIY publishing have become more accessible. I think it's totally worth it in those ways.

I'm in a weird small public position, where I get emails from people all over the world saying, "I've never heard about these ideas before, but I saw an interview you did and they make sense." It's not me, creating a cult of personality; it's that I'm talking about these ideas in accessible ways and in mediums where people who aren't exposed to them can find them. I think there is some power of shifting culture in that. That these ideas can still make it through all of those media filters. Some anarchists kick me for talking to media, saying that I'm defanging and mainstreaming these ideas. I think there is some legitimate critique there, but it misses out on bigger picture engagement. That sometimes ideas become too big for the clubhouse and reach more people no matter what. There is always a tension as ideas move from the subcultures and the margins to mainstream. They do get watered down, or can lose their original intention or transform from the meanings they started with. I think that's inevitable with any ideas. They have life cycles. Richard Dawkins compared ideas to cultural memes, as something that self-replicates, grows, and transforms as it's passed within civil society. All ideas—or memes—eventually take on lives of their own that no one has control of—even Power or corporations or grassroots social movements.

But the thing is, my engagements with big media are rarely to sort all the variations or depths of anarchy out. I have done that in creating new media and through social media. My role has often been like other anarchists like Cindy Milstein or David Graeber, to talk about these ideas in accessible ways and offer counter-narratives to the mainstream, then let other people decide what they want to do with them. I'm not the brightest bulb, but I seem to be able to connect people with ideas that have often been portrayed as scary.

MT: The ideas of anarchism scare many people. It takes a lot of time and patience to show others what it has to offer, and building counter-narratives is hard work. Can you talk about that?

sc: First, I think it's important to see media with a bigger view as a sort of landscape with many different places spread across it. 'Media' can mean so much, from social sites, to self-publishing, to newspapers and TV, for example. Then remember that within this larger media landscape, that shifting culture takes time. Rarely will a single article or piece of coverage have big impact on its own, especially a counter-narrative that goes against the grain. It takes the ideas appearing across many news outlets from small local papers and weeklies to cable and network TV reinforcing variations of themes for a 'media consensus' to emerge. People have to be exposed multiple times for ideas to take root. So we have to look at media communication in a wider sense.

This is what the 'professional' public relations industry does every day, except they are selling crap ideas and products to manipulate us all. It's hard to challenge those lies if we don't think in terms of creating our own counter-narratives, or telling our own collective stories throughout the whole media landscape, both big and small. Often activist media trainings only teach people the first steps, like how to have 'talking points' to spoon feed the media a message without getting off point, but it's ineffective if the messages only happen once or twice. What I want people to do is similar, except think of it in larger recurring themes that get repeated in many different ways, across many places over a period of time. A rudimentary example is, I often say within media is that anarchists don't want a kinder, gentler capitalism; we don't want it at all. I don't say it the same way, but it's something I try to get in to the narrative as much as possible no matter what the subject of the article is. That would be a counter-narrative in big media, because often capitalism and its baggage is never even challenged at all. It's just assumed it's the way things are. I believe we have to write our own stories for ourselves and for others. And what is seen as a counter-narrative in big media is just a narrative when we are creating our own media. I don't see them as that much different, as much as how they are presented. The only difference is, in a subculture we can use a shorthand language to muddle through abstract ideas, whereas presenting them to a wider group takes changing some of the language to explain them.

If I, or someone, gets interviewed, journalists are going to get some things right, more often, they're going to get some things wrong. That's what a lot of activists and groups' limited experiences are: "Oh, the media gets it wrong every time." But what I recognize is, when you tell your narratives a lot, you start to have this mapping of them across the media landscape. They get enough of the pieces right that you start to have this larger conversation emerge. If you stay true to what you're saying, not just talking points, but if you stay within the realm, then all of a sudden you have shaped the counter-narrative in a much larger context. If I talk to a paper in

Idaho, and then I talk to the Huffington Post in D.C., they're all going to get some things right. When I put it onto my website, and somebody looks at it, people read those articles and there are themes of ideas that start to emerge that I want to emerge out of them, because I am constantly consciously engaging the media in shaping the narratives. I don't want to sound Machiavellian, but it's just smart media work. I find that mapping, that the media landscape as I call it, is way more powerful in shifting culture and ideas than any single interview or article could ever be.

MT: So far, we've been talking about mainstream commercial news media. What about social media, which many activists now embrace?

sc: Let me talk about social media as part of what's often called *new media*, which to me basically means any form of media that allows people or groups to get their messages out, or to converse without the control or filters of big media. New Media is mostly digitally based, but it can include self-publishing zines or books, DIY videos, smart phones, blogs, and individual sites for example. I see new media as representative of powerful decentralized platforms for individuals, groups, and communities to tell their own stories on their own terms in shifting culture and creating counter-narratives for sure. It's not necessarily profit-driven, but often can interact with media owned by corporations. New media allows for stories that can be in-depth or personal, or have deep analysis that big media filters would never allow. It allows people to engage in dialogs that just aren't available through other traditional channels and are places to create counter-narratives, often ignored, left out, or marginalized by dinosaur media.

Which is often why big media has figured out to pay attention to it, even if any individual outlet or person doesn't have millions of eyeballs on it. There is still collective influence or consensus that emerges quickly. Memes spread through social media can grow rapidly and change the discourse of stories and opinions. Often now breaking stories appear through new media before big media can catch up. I have seen this repeatedly over the last few years. Someday new media will just be media, but the divide is big for now.

When I talk about new media, social media is absolutely part of it, but new media encompasses much more. Social media are the familiar platforms that many people worldwide use daily like Facebook, Tumblr, Twitter, etc. Most of them are corporate controlled with few exceptions. Social media has been a boon for anarchists and social movements because it has opened unprecedented ability to connect and organize in real time which has arguably changed the course of recent political uprisings and ideas internationally. I cannot deny its been a huge paradigm shifting force at least for now in terms of isolated people being able to connect and again reach others without the old media gatekeepers. An example is the issues of police brutality and police killing innocent people has come under intense scrutiny because of the spread of messages and video so quickly. All of the sudden isolated events now can be seen as patterns no matter what the 'official' record says. This kind of mapping was impossible before except by experts or people with access to obscure databases.

We already know the pitfalls of big media, but new and social media have them, too. If I can talk about some brief points. The first is that new media can create a bubble or echo chamber of like-minded voices, especially in the corporate-controlled social media spheres like Twitter. Stories or issues can seem to have more consensus or be bigger than they might really be because of this reverberation amongst similar viewpoints. This is a double-edged sword, in that people can find affinity and comfort if they've been in the wilderness of ideas, they can find a choir to join. The flipside of that is that often people won't or don't look outside of that choir, or worse, refuse to critically listen to voices outside of it which creates confirmation bias. I've heard this referred to as the *filter bubble* or *internet siloing*.[1]

Also places like Facebook or Google have become the greatest data information gathering places that our world has ever known. The NSA, the FBI's, or CIA's databases on activists pale in comparison and are far less comprehensive than what we all willingly share online. So in grassroots political organizing there is always an equation that has to be weighed out on the use of social media as an organizing tool between our transparency and the potential blow back of that. I personally opt for transparency in the public sphere—but not stupidly—because I have found protection in it. Obviously people have to weigh it out for any given time or situation.

Another thing to think about is that all electronic media is so evaporative. It rarely has staying power because it comes in and out so quickly. Stories, ideas, and topics can move through without much reflection, then sort of disappear into the cacophony of internet buzz. I think knowing that, it's important in crafting counter-narratives that we continually put those ideas back into the new media sphere or into some of the old school ways like print. Online articles disappear hourly and sometimes they need longer shelf lives. So asking how people can create that longevity in new media is important.

Lastly, social media today is largely sold to us and treated by us as a modern day commons. The new social gathering places. But the reality is that those sites are largely corporate-controlled and we are treated as data for them to advertise to. All of them have taken the public trust and commodified us. I only say this for people to think about for the future. Can they limit speech? Will they charge us? If these are the new commons what does that say about our interactions or deeper connections with each

1   Internet Silos https://edge.org/response-detail/23777; Filter Bubble https://en.wikipedia.org/wiki/Filter_bubble

other? These kinds of questions we won't be able to answer for a while.

MT: You're pretty hard on corporate media, but at the same time you're adept at using it to present anarchist ideas. It seems like there might be a tension there. Can you tell me about your experience with the *New York Times*?

sc: Sure. Let me give a little background. I was under surveillance by the FBI, as an alleged *terrorist*, from at least about 1999 to 2008. The Austin People's Legal Collective, an Austin group at the time, filed a Freedom of Information Act request for me to these agencies. I got hundreds of pages of documents out of possible thousands, which revealed that I had been under nationwide and borderline illegal surveillance by the Feds. I couldn't sue the FBI for crossing the line or having my rights violated because I was not denied employment or schooling, even though I did nothing.

So, what could I do? I could talk to the media! I could use the power of the media to tell a narrative. I approached somebody at the *New York Times* that I had built a rapport with, who had used me as a source. Not an anonymous source—they had quoted me before. I had built a friendly rapport with them over four years as a reliable source to talk about anarchism, surveillance, etc. We weren't close. This was just somebody I had a contact with if they were talking about anarchism in a piece, they could say, "Hey, what's an anarchist take on this? Can I quote you on this?" So, I would do that—not as 'the' anarchist voice, but 'an' anarchist voice.

I approached him with the documents and said, "Are you interested in writing about this as a vehicle to talk about the wider surveillance that is going on?" This was in 2010, before Edward Snowden's leaked documents broke. There were a few articles in big media on surveillance that were coming out, but not much yet. The *Times* saw the potential in this. Since I had been working on media for decades I knew I could ask for certain points to be made. It doesn't mean they will happen, but is worth asking. I said, "I want three things to come out of this article: I want the ideas of anarchy to seem reasonable and rational. I want to seem reasonable and rational. And I want the FBI to look as stupid, as they really are." Now, the *New York Times* is not my mouthpiece. They're not going to do it my way. But because I had those three points, I was able to have some influence in shaping that, as far as that was concerned, in my limited scope through telling them, and reinforcing it in my answers to their questions. Whereas before, they would just quote you and you have nothing to say with it. The writers Colin Moynihan and Scott Shane worked on the piece for nine months before it was published. The article came out and I 'won' on all three of those points—even as they got everything wrong. [laughs] They didn't represent anarchy the way I wanted it to be, but they didn't make it sound like chaos and destruction, either. I came off as very reasonable and rational. And the FBI, due to their own maleficence, their own bad work, came off looking like jackasses. That article had a huge amount of influence in spreading the ideas of anarchy, of making people reassess the surveillance state that we are under, and that I was a rational person to talk about these ideas.

MT: It was page A1 in the *Times*.

sc: Exactly. I mean, the *New York Times* put anarchy in a positive light on the front page. Now, they got kicked by the right-wing media for it, and again, they got a lot of things wrong. So that was an example of where I tried that. And yes, it was absolutely successful for what it was. That article helped to put surveillance on the international map since it was picked up by almost every paper across the US and abroad. People in big cities and small towns were talking about unfettered surveillance. Then everyone was able to take in the info because the corporate media, the *Times* of record had written about it. And then other people wrote articles around it, because of that article. At the time, Vice or the Huffington Post could never have that kind of reach. So it was a very powerful medium in that way.

I recognized that it was a platform to talk about these ideas that were relegated to these corners that nobody talked about on an international scale. An unknown anarchist from Texas could help bring this to light. It was one of the pieces along with the indie documentary films *Better this World, Informant,* and *If a Tree Falls* that set the stage for the surveillance conversation to emerge widely when the Snowden leaks broke. Then spying couldn't be swept under the rug by government or corporations anymore. They had to answer questions and the public perception absolutely turned against blanket spying. People questioned the use of informants, the entrapment, and targeting of Muslims and activists in the US.

The way I treated all of that was a conscious effort. This was after 20 years of working with the media. There's such a rudimentary misunderstanding about the way media works amongst activists, anarchists, and radicals. A lot of times we have these trainings where people get basic media skills, like *flipping the script* or having your talking points. But they never really develop an analysis about the power of media. Having gone through those things, I sort of developed this larger, deeper analysis about media and recognizing the power of the forms of media.

A lot of radicals and activists don't ever see it that way. A lot of anarchists are very combative to corporate or big media unless they're creating their own media. What I'm saying is, "Look, let's use it to whatever advantage we can have, knowing that it has limits to it. And at the same time, tell our own stories our own way." It's never going to be what we want, but we *can* shape it.

One of the biggest manifestations of using media to tell our own narratives was at the Common Ground Collective in New Orleans. I already knew the power or narratives then. We worked corporate media to tell all these stories about what a great relief organization we were, how there were these dirty anarchists working in it, so that they could absorb it. But at the same time, we worked with grassroots media to tell about building this radical stuff, this revolution that we were building in New Orleans—not for ourselves, but with the people of New Orleans, for the people of New Orleans and the Gulf Coast. We were able to work both of these, so we were able to appeal to large groups of people. Radicals and anarchists would come, and also at the same time regular people who could support it.

That was a conscious media strategy. We didn't write it down, but that was a conscious media strategy for a handful of us to do. And we worked it for a long time. That's part of the reason why it attracted so many people and why there's thousands of articles about Common Ground Collective.

One of the things I think, too, that a lot of activists run into is that not only are they combative, they don't recognize the power of media. They want it to be fair. They want it to tell the truth. And really, in my analysis, we are engaged in propaganda wars. The state, Power, corporations will never tell the truth. They can't. They don't even know how to tell the truth. The bureaucracies in it will never let it happen. The mechanisms of Power will never let "the truth" come out, especially with the influence of corporations and their secret front groups, their PR firms, and all the shitty things that they do behind the scenes to make their clients look good.

So, why do we want to just tell the truth? Because the truth is not enough against the distortions, the lies, and misrepresentations. Just because we have some truth are we going to be some kind of shining light, a beacon? No. Truth is not enough in the media. It's a complicated fight over stories. It doesn't mean we have to lie or distort things. There's enough truth on our side to be real, and to emphasize them, but we need to develop good stories and tell them to combat the professional PR in big media and within our own communities. They will never tell the truth and will do everything in their power to distort anything that doesn't fit their agenda. This group Smartmeme calls it the 'battle of the story'. I think professional NGOs recognized the power of the story a long time ago, but a lot of grassroots organizations and grassroots activists don't.

MT: I'm not sure the truth will actually matter in some of these battles. You get the truth out there, then what?

sc: I agree. The truth doesn't matter, and what is 'truth' anyway? So let's quit pretending media is objective and that our enemies will play fair. It's sadly a win-lose situation a lot of times when we engage and people or groups have to weigh it out, but if they do there is much to gain in sharing liberatory ideas.

//

Matt Tedrow is an independent journalist and recently received his Ph.D. in Media Studies.

METHODS
AND
PROPOSALS

A CONVERSATION IN THREE ACTS

By Kit O'Connell

Originally appeared serially on Firedog Lake; February 2014

Part 1: OCCUPY & ACTIVISM

One reason I wanted to chat with scott crow was his experience with Common Ground Collective in New Orleans. In recent years, we've seen similar collectives spring out of the activist networks formed by Occupy Wall Street—projects like Occupy Sandy. Late last year, alongside key Common Ground Collective organizer Lisa Fithian and many others, I organized Austin Common Ground Relief to respond to a record-breaking flood on Halloween. As the group's dispatcher, I relied on the networks and skills formed during Occupy Austin.

Kit O'Connell: There's always been activism happening but the last few years it seems there's been more activity, more people in the streets, more stuff happening. Do you agree?

scott crow: Yeah, we have had lots of ruptures, where things kind of jump off and revolutionary potential has risen, followed by lulls, the in-between times since the millennium. Its been like a sine wave where it rises and falls. Right now its been volatile, especially since Occupy. So in the twenty plus years I've been doing activism and engaged with community organizing in local, national, and international struggles, I've seen a lot of ruptures and lulls. When I came back in really seriously to organizing was in the alternative globalization movement, the post-Seattle stuff. When that kicked off it was huge! We could get 10,000 people to a demonstration internationally with the summit hopping that was going on.

After September 11 it sort of died down. But then the wars kicked off. And I don't mean the War on the Poor or the War on Women, but the international wars. And in that you saw another rupture where thousands of people were in the streets.

And then it kind of leveled off and then we were struck with some pretty serious disasters. One was the man-made and natural disaster of Hurricane Katrina. That actually drew a lot of people to it, which was another form of a rupture. Because then people came to the Gulf Coast by the hundreds of thousands, literally.

Then there was a lull, but then we come to the next disaster, which was the economic collapse of 2008. All of these things have been brewing since the millennium as capitalism's been in crisis which lead to Occupy. And it's just a natural progression of all this. So that was just the latest rupture to happen.

It's always interesting to watch—the way I actually look at it is like an ocean with currents that produce waves that building, which represents the ruptures, then they just finally crest and crash into the shore to recede back. What's left on the shore are the lulls. The lull is when we reflect and heal to make our next steps. Then what I like to see is what happen in the lulls, in between the ruptures, right—what comes out of it? So when the rupture happens there's thousands—I just want to be clear I'm not saying 'the Rapture!' [laughs]

The tensions are the highest and when the people are the most. We saw in the Occupy movements, it was incredibly beautiful, internationally, but definitely in the states, all across the country. But then it starts to recede and we see who's left and what projects come out of it, because that helps us build for the next level.

I think that what came out of the Occupy movements was a really beautiful rupture, because you'd already seen the largest influence of anarchy and anarchist ideas in the modern times since the time of Emma Goldman and the IWW and people back then. We're in an anarchist renaissance. So when people came into Occupy, they came in with these horizontal organizing ideas, the ideas of participatory democracy, the ideas of direct action, without even thinking about it. And that's forty years of organizing for a lot of people in the United States, but for me that's twenty years of engagement—not that I was a part of all of it, but seeing it all come to fruition.

KO: What about the push back against it all from the media or from people who just wanted it to be the Democratic answer to the Tea Party in addition to all the cooptation?

SC: Those tensions are always there. There's always people and groups trying to pilfer off of social and political ruptures, trying to suck them like vampires for their own power, influence, or agendas. The labor unions, the Democrats, nonprofits, professional media, etcetera, there's a long history of that. And back in the day it used to be Communists who would have been in the mix trying to control it too. [laughs]

And then there's the political immaturity that permeates the US. The country that forgets history, or hell, yesterday, that wants to hang onto the power structures that got us into these predicaments in the first place. If we could vote our way out, don't you think people would have already done it? The political immaturity is not about age, but experience, analysis, and practice at engagements outside of 'normal' channels. It takes exposure and practice to unlock all the baggage because we never get a chance too. Those two elements destroy and subvert movement's liberatory potential on all sides of the spectrum.

For all the problems of things like Occupy general assemblies for example often being chaotic therapy sessions, its still a chance for people to stretch their voices despite the vampires and the lack of exposure.

PART 2: MUTUAL AID

KO: You mentioned projects that appear during lulls. I see Occupy Sandy, or the Austin Common Ground Relief work we did here recently and all that ties into what you were doing at Common Ground Collective. Mutual aid is good for its own sake, but how do we connect that politically? We don't want to turn anyone off. We don't want to politicize our aid but our aid is political. How do we make that connection? What happens next after an Occupy Sandy?

sc: I think it only is what it is. You can only 'politicize' it as much as you can. I think what's really important is the culture we create internally within our political and social movements and also the way we engage outwardly with other people—though it's more permeable than that. We're not trying to convert people to anarchy or to communism or whatever it is—although communists did try to convert people just like religious wingnuts. Really, what we do is you just make [anarchism] make sense to people while supporting them in getting back on their feet, then they can determine their own futures. When you go to help someone and you name it mutual aid, people see that in real life and real time. Unfortunately, that's the only way to do it. There is no conversion.

It's the idea of attraction, not the idea of conversion. That actually comes out of Alcoholics Anonymous, I didn't make that up. The aid work is something which just emerges sort of by accident out of all these projects. Like at Common Ground Collective in New Orleans and the Gulf Coast, we were able to pull from the alternative globalization movement: street medics, indymedia, and Food Not Bombs, and all these things which had been going on were brought to the Gulf.

KO: These were networks built through activism that then were pulled in for aid.

sc: Yes. We didn't consciously say, 'Hey, we're going to do this for aid!' Now we're starting to see that this has become a newer model, another point of intersection against the crisis of capitalism and climate change. Make it as political as possible without drawing fake lines: like "we're anarchist and you're not." Or, "this is radical and you're not." And also just being honest about who we are. I don't want to convert anyone.

KO: But you're honest about where you're coming from.

sc: Absolutely! I told people I was an anarchist from the beginning in New Orleans. And these are people, in some communities, who had hardly ever seen white people. I'm literally serious about that. They'd say "I've barely seen white people except on TV. You're an anarchist, what is that? And why are you here?" Now they'll tell you, "The anarchists came. No one else showed up, but the anarchists came." I'm sure your experience with Austin Common Ground was maybe not as extreme, but similar.

KO: Sure, I had some people who took me aside who were like "I get what you guys are doing here." We didn't avoid talking about our politics, people knew we were organizers but it was never about that, obviously. It was about "here's a meal." During some of the later events in December, people told me, "We will remember you and what you did."

sc: It's also about connecting things. So when you're gutting somebody's house, you can come in like a service organization and say, "Yeah, we're going to gut your house. Then we're going to go on to do something else." That's the charity model. But if you come in with the solidarity model, it's like, "We're doing this because we want you to get back on your feet, because we want you to build your own community power the way you see fit." Then not jumping to the next crisis, but staying around for the long haul. It's a different way to approach it. I don't care if we name them as anarchy or solidarity or not. It's not a brand. There's no gain in it. It's just a point of reference, at least to me, in the way we engage with each other.

Part 3: Technology and Intersectionality

One important tool which defines modern activism is the use of social media for organizing and building solidarity. While social media does little unless paired with "meatspace" direct action, it can be a powerful tool for motivating people, reporting on live events, and building intersectional movements that address multiple issues like hierarchy, patriarchy, or racism, for instance, simultaneously across geography. When arrests first occurred at Occupy Austin, we heard from activists in Egypt who had staged an impromptu protest at the US Embassy.

Between times of "rupture," social media becomes even more crucial for strengthening solidarity and relating about core issues. This can be seen in recent, vital discussions on Twitter over race, feminism, and the meaning and origins of Occupy. Likewise, more people are using social media and the Internet to educate themselves about politics and current events. To close our conversation, I asked scott crow how he thought social media was changing our political conversations.

KO: The word 'anarchy' or 'socialism' used to be these hot button words that could be used to turn people off. You used those words and people's minds closed down. The mainstream media and the politicians use this constantly.

"Obama's a socialist!" But it doesn't seem to be working anymore. People are less likely to believe you. Why do you think that's happening?

sc: Because people are smart. And they can see that it's propaganda. Even if they don't have a 'political analysis' they can see that it's total bullshit. Can I say bullshit? [laughs] Also, it's access to incredible amounts of information that people didn't have before.

I think you're totally right about the jargon. The thing is—with words like that—I can't speak to socialism because it did get such a sort of deserved bad rap for so long. But anarchy was always assumed to be chaos and bomb-throwing. But because anarchy is the largest set of ideas in ascension in social justice movements—in the US, Canada, Mexico, even Europe—more than Communism (big C Communism). The *New York Times* and CNN, they can't ignore it or malign it anymore because of social media and people's access to other forms of news. Sure, anarchists are out in the streets in black bloc, throwing tear gas canisters back when they are shot at them by the police, but they are also at the front lines of disaster relief, they're at the front lines of occupying and reclaiming spaces that should be the commons—you can't deny that. We are health practitioners, day care workers, farmers, teachers, we serve your coffee, we are everywhere. You can't knock it off to a fringe element and people can see that clearly. We're in an anarchist renaissance—there's more anarchist literature produced in English in the last 14 years than there had been in the previous 50 or 60 years in the United States and even internationally.

Anarchy went underground. People stopped talking about it. They started to hide in other organizations. It reemerged in the '60s but still at the fringes. But now there's a huge body of work—more books have come out, more articles are written now. And the internet helps with that because it is an open platform itself to talk about ideas and actions without the old media filters, because if you're in Idaho or Texas or New York, you can be connected and share ideas.

KO: That leads into the intersectionality that's happening. That's not a new concept obviously but the Internet seems to promote it. In my view, when Occupy worked best was when it was its most intersectional.

sc: Absolutely. That's the thing that attracted me to anarchy originally. I came to it later in my life in my late twenties, but anarchy was the only political philosophy that seemed to embrace intersectionality and connecting the struggles. That all issues were important—what was happening in prisons, in the environment, with animals, rape culture, what happened outwardly but also inwardly—in how we treat each other; that these are interlinked forms of oppression. While a lot of movements are about converting people to their single issue, party, their line, their nonprofit. Anarchists and feminists were drawing connections to all the forms of exploitation and oppression.

You bring up a point that needs to be reiterated. I think the internet is very conducive to that. It's almost like a buffet—where you can see something about animal liberation and then something about prisons right below it in your news feed. And you say, 'Oh yeah, those are both important.'

KO: But intersectionality seems like a key to growing any kind of movement right now. And on the ground, doing the work it can seem really obvious. How is Palestine linked to Capitalism? Because Capitalism props that occupation up. But then it becomes time to regurgitate that into a sound bite and that's where it starts to break down. I'm a journalist, so maybe I shouldn't say this, but maybe that's not so necessary. We don't always have to make our messages packageable for the media.

sc: I think you do both. You make sound bites for old dinosaur media, but you write and talk in more depth in new media where the internet and alternative forms of media opens up a space for that. I've done interviews recently—it used to be you just got the quote, you got the sound bite, but I've done interviews now that are 10 or 15 or 20,000 words. I really like that kind of news because I want to digest news. I'm not saying everything has to be belabored, it's fine to have a *listicle* like Top Ten Reasons to Overthrow Capitalism or whatever. But I do like that I can find really in depth articles now that maybe appeared only rarely before in *Rolling Stone* or *Esquire*.

KO: Tell me about what you're working on now.

sc: I have a few books in the works due out in the next couple of years covering various topics including: an anthology on the history and praxis of community armed self defense, a memoir of living under FBI surveillance for a decade, and a book for activists on moving from a politics of opposition to a politics of possibilities. I also am working with an anarchist PR firm called *Agency* and sitting on the advisory committee of Treasure City Thrift.[1] Oh yeah, and traveling speaking a lot!

That's what I'm working on. Then I'm meeting with good folks like yourselves and having good conversations in between. Not that exciting is it? Used to be I'm going down to this lock-down or this action, I'm not doing that anymore.

KO: You're tired of going to jail?

sc: Jail I don't even mind, at all. Actually I organize every time I'm in jail, but it has to be for something bigger to make it worth going back. I won't do it just for a single reform issue or activist points. I'll let others fill that role if they want. [laughs] Speaking broadly,

---

1   *Agency* http://www.anarchistagency.com; Treasure City Thrift http://www.treasurecitythrift.org

activists often use arrests as badge of commitment to 'the cause' when I might argue there are more important things to do with the limited resources we have amongst us—time, money and people.

KO: It's got to be a big moment.

sc: Absolutely!

//

Kit O'Connell is a gonzo journalist who is openly biased toward human rights and equality. He writes and edits for a number of independent journals from Austin, Texas.

THE LIBERATORY POTENTIAL OF WORKER CO-OPS:
A Look at Ecology Action and Treasure City Thrift

By Anne Gessler
Originally appeared in The Cooperative Oral History Project
January 2012

Anne Gessler: Describe a little bit about what led you to cooperative/collective process here in Austin. What were your childhood experiences that led you to embrace that?

scott crow: I think it has always been instilled in me—I grew up working class poor, and there was always this thing in our family about sharing, even when you had little to nothing. I think that innately we are collaborators and that we cooperate to survive. Even in my youngest days I was willing to take whatever I had—my peanut butter sandwich and give away half of it if it was needed. It's been a long process-awakenings along the way. I've always felt that there's enough pie to go around, especially in this country and that we should share. Those ideas didn't come out of political philosophies—but of innate cultural experience; politics just gave them names.

As I grew up in the scene of punk and industrial music in the '80s with bands like Consolidated, Swans, Skinny Puppy and Ministry—who we toured/did shows with—really influenced me. They exposed me to political and philosophical concepts. The band functioned cooperatively when we toured. We made all band decisions collectively. We booked events in these places where you don't know people and had to trust that they'd pay you; then we would divide what little money there was equally. It worked out great most of the time. Those rudimentary forms of mutual aid and power sharing-anarchy were the foundation of my understanding.

In the early '90s I went into the antique business and was in for almost 10 years. I did business with people around the country based on handshakes or promise of a word. There's this *huge* underground economy in the antique world that's based on cooperation. In Dallas, in 1995, I co-founded an art gallery co-op, then an antique worker co-op with four other people. We got together because we wanted to share space, resources, and labor. In all of this there was not a real political overtone or undertone to it. It made sense to collectively make decisions and share resources and responsibilities. This was another one of the places before I became an anarchist where I saw mutual aid or cooperation take place. Later, identifying as an anarchist and the political model of what we were doing really made sense.

Growing up I didn't see a lot of anarchists except in our small, early '80s punk rock scene. And those guys were assholes. In 1998 I was reintroduced to anarchist ideas. I met some people and started to really come to understand the deeper ideas and history of anarchism. I felt like I had been given cultural and political references to practices that were already part of my life, ideas like mutual aid and direct action. I call it little "a" anarchism because it's not a rigid set of ideas. To me it was so beautiful. Anarchist ideas weren't just *against* everything, it could be about *building* and *creating* alternatives, too, like imagining worlds that were beyond capitalism and cooperatives in general became part of that.

Around '96–'97 a lot of anarchists started to flock to Austin. Through the '90s many anarchist influenced currents and movements were rising. There were people working on alternative globalization, radical animal rights, and environmental issues. There was train hopping and music, as well as remnants of the '70s Austin radical and cooperative projects. All came crashing upon the shores with new life in 2000 after the WTO in Seattle.

I moved to Austin in 2001 to take part in existing projects, unlike in Dallas where we'd always had to build everything from the ground up. Austin had giant black flags waving and Black Bloc contingents at every big demonstration. In addition, there were all these horizontally run cooperative and collective projects.

Some key anarchist projects in Austin were going on, and many still are. The Yellow Bike Project, which gives out free bikes and teaches people repairs started in the mid '90s. The Inside Books Project, which gives free books to prisoners, got started in the '90s. There's Ecology Action, which is the oldest environmental organization and oldest worker co-op in Texas. It was started in 1970 as a volunteer collective, but turned into a traditional nonprofit in '78. It returned to a horizontal worker co-op in 2000. Monkeywrench Books, a collectively run radical bookstore started in 2001. Now defunct the Rhizome Collective was a huge warehouse space and hub that started in 2000 which nested a lot of organizations within—Indymedia, Bikes Across Borders, a lending library, permaculture gardens, Food Not Bombs—all were housed, at one point or another, at the Rhizome. A few of these projects had paid staff, but most were/are volunteer collectives. Then, after 2006, a group of us began a whole new wave of trying to start horizontal worker cooperatives specifically to create jobs with dignity and a living wage and to fund projects that no one else would, like Inside Books.

AG: Can you tell me a little about co-ops?

sc: In brief, it's a structure for people to share decision making powers and resources in deciding their futures, whether it's in work, housing, land, or food. It's supposed to create liberation from traditional structures. There are all different kinds of co-ops; consumer, labor, housing, agricultural, worker, and credit unions. The most frequently seen are consumer food co-ops and credit unions. Worker cooperatives are one of the smallest sectors within co-ops. The cooperative movements first took root in the United States in the 1800s. They've risen in bad economic times and fallen in good times over time. The '60s–'70s saw the last big cooperative boom until now. Today there are thousands across North America. I would even argue that there are more co-ops and volunteer collectives than there ever has been in recent world history.

I would attribute this to the failures of capitalism, communism, and socialism and partially to the undercurrent of anarchism that has emerged from many grassroots currents due to those failures. I mention anarchism because just look at what's happening with the Occupy Movement and all the trends since 1999.

It is important to note that Occupy have general assemblies, make decisions by consensus, and are trying to be as leaderless as possible. All of these elements are evidence of the last 20 years, at least, of anarchist ideas in the US The anarchists are pushing the new horizontal worker cooperatives paradigm too. Horizontal worker cooperatives are the largest growing sector within this. In traveling nationally, I get to see how small worker cooperatives segments are growing with mostly young people in their 20s and 30s forming them At my ripe old age of 44, [laughs] which I still consider young, I often find myself to be one of the oldest people involved.

The reason I am excited about horizontal worker co-ops is that I think they are the only form of co-ops actually engaged in collective liberation and thinking beyond just creating job alternatives within our economic system. Many co-ops which include housing, agricultural, and food aren't actually democratic or engaged in power sharing. That doesn't make them *not* democratic, but only *marginally* democratic. Co-ops are not necessarily in opposition to capitalism. They're actually pretty ingrained within it or an alternative within it.

There are some underlying issues that co-ops will need to address. Consumer co-ops, like credit unions for example, with thousands of members, are often no better than a bank, although it has this implied local or democratic value in it. It's still finance. Financial deals are not going to be made on a handshake with a membership that has 30,000 people in it. There is no community connection. Their money isn't going to stay in that community. It's going to travel trans-nationally, just like banks, due to their ties to international financial institutions.

Then there are worker cooperatives which lead toward more democratic openings. Being worker-owners you have say in your life, which is good, but even within worker co-ops there are two distinct schools of thought. There's the traditional hierarchy of worker co-ops and then there are the horizontal ones emerging. The hierarchical ones look just very much like traditional business models, except that the worker-owners all have some limited power within it—but they can still have a boss. Some of them have different pay scales. The ratio may be 1 to 3, 5, or 6 between the lowest and highest paid. While some are as high as 1 to 10. We can say that's better than a CEO who has 1 to 450 or 4,050. But does that make it better or only more economical? Most of the traditional co-ops say 'One member, one vote', but if you're a manager, you still wield unrecognized power within the organization. This is true for a lot of worker co-ops that started in the '60s and '70s.

My focus is on horizontal worker cooperatives, where there are elements of job sharing, equalized power distribution and where the pay scale, benefits, and management are flat. I'm not saying that this is the only way, but if there is work and pay for labor this is one of the best options. All of the worker co-ops I have been part of or co-founded, including Ecology Action, worked like that. It was easier because we were small, but what do you do when there are 200 people? I don't have the answer for that—except maybe not creating workplaces that have such large employment.

Through my work in small worker co-ops I have been fortunate to see success in minimizing hierarchy and unequal power dynamics and in creating just and democratic workplaces that treat people with dignity. Co-ops aren't going to revolutionize civil society, but they may be part of better transitions and building counter power. They haven't always been perfect, but they have allowed us to challenge the dominant ideas of how economies and power sharing intersect.

AG: How much influence or links do you see as holdovers from the 1960s and 1970s Austin cooperative movements in Austin's current worker and volunteer collectives?

sc: Not much, outside of Ecology Action, which had been through many phases. There had been this project called Austin Community Project (ACP), an ambitious, visionary set of volunteer and cooperative projects which existed from 1975 to 1978. Sadly we didn't know about ACP when we were reinventing the wheel again! [laughs]

I'll digress for a minute. One of the problems within larger socio-political movements is that we often forget or devalue the past. The *cliché* that history repeats itself rings true as new people come into social or political consciousness making the same mistakes or come to the same great ideas without having looked at the past. It's often assumed that this moment in time is the only relevant one, as we reinvent the same wheel. When I talk to people who are newer to movements I say that you've *got* to look at history. Not that everything was done right or see the actors as heroic, but look at history because there are pieces that we can learn from and actually use.

While we were laying plans for our great idea of a 'mutual aid network' [laughs] some friends dug up the documents on the Austin Community Project. Seeing those documents was like reading our own notes. Austin Community Project was vibrant, at one point up to forty different projects working within it. It looked like it had about 200 people involved at varying capacities running small farms, forming worker co-ops, health centers, recycling and food co-ops, transportation and more. But they suffered from the same chronic problems of bottom up grassroots organizing due to the machines of capital. There was a lack of resources, time, money and people. So many things are done haphazardly on shoestring budgets.

It was nice to see that we were part of some historical tradition with shared ideas, values and principles, (and problems) others had before in our town. They left no legacy except those documents and now, thirty five years later, what exists? Two co-ops. Wheatsville, the grocery store and Ecology Action, the recycling center which had already existed, are all that's left.

When we did review those documents, the radical history of the ACP did help us understand at least two valuable lessons:

First we started to look to the past because we were trying to build not just individual cooperatives but we wanted to integrate them into systems. We thought we had this great idea, we're going to integrate projects, like, production, manufacturing, transportation, distribution, service, health care, education, and cultural programs. All these integrated parts, because we wanted to create alternative economies and power—not just alternative businesses within a capitalist economy. We said, "I'm sure someone has done this before," because we knew that the Spanish Anarchists did it in the '20s and '30s, and definitely stepped it up during the Civil War. We *knew* someone else had done it along the way. Then those ACP documents came to us.

Second, that even long-term planning without resources is always going to be difficult and challenging. There are just not a lot of mechanisms in place to support radical co-ops yet, like, traditional funding. There are a lot more hurdles to get over including funding, laws, and liberal culture.

AG: Is there a community of cooperatives and collectives in Austin now or is it more pluralistic?

SC: Today it's a loose network. We tried to formalized it into a spokes-council about a year ago with mixed success, and the 'mutual aid network' never materialized beyond a couple of projects, but we realized that most of the new worker co-ops that are getting off the ground are too busy to do that. There's talk of getting it going once again. Since we started this endeavor we've lost two co-ops while a couple of the others became much more stable and bigger. It's hard to get a business going, especially when you consciously want to start a worker co-op that's horizontally run. You're not only starting a business, which is difficult, but mixing these liberatory cultural, social, and political pieces that just adds layers of complexity to what you're doing. For example, if you want a horizontal wage, you have to figure out how to make enough money to pay everyone equally, instead of just one person making money and paying people crappy wages to work for them. Putting all of these efforts into the workplace or volunteer spaces eats up much of the spirit and time, leaving less energy to organize with the other groups.

AG: Thinking about the way you relate to other people from different ethnicities or cultures or genders, or sexual identities. How do you, even as you work toward this alternative economy, also try to foment change within people—the actual worker-members of the collective—to change their ingrained social biases or prejudices?

sc: In all the cooperatives and collectives I have engaged in since 2000, we consciously sought to create cultures within them that address issues like overlapping and disparate communities, power sharing, privilege, and oppression and recognizing mistakes through the anarchist framework of collective liberation. Collective liberation recognizes that there are historical and systemic inequalities in our economic, political, and cultural systems that favor some over others, that commodify all of us and the natural world. These principles have provided a framework to reduce those hierarchies and dynamics while still being in the systems.

Everything in our lives, politically, socially, culturally—shapes and brings us to each moment in our lives. This includes family dynamics, our workplaces, race, sexual identities, geography, and our economic location in civil society. If we want to have a culture based on collective liberation, then we must bring all those aspects to the surface to subvert them.

Another important piece is to give ourselves permission to stumble and fall, because we all do and will. We are making this up as we go so let's be kind to ourselves and each other along the way as we learn and exercise power. It's all part of the process. It isn't easier, but is a lot more rewarding.

There is no one 'community' but each of us is part of multiple, overlapping communities. The fluidity opens up the possibility to meet people where they're at.

For example, Ecology Action, where I work, is a place where we experiment with all of this in real time. In 25 years of work in many organizations, I've never worked at one organization that's had so much good will and was able to cross so many boundaries—from street people to the halls of Power, in all sections of civil society, including those of us who are outside of the state. It's been amazing to watch.

I was brought in to Ecology Action to bring these ideas because the current collective wanted to develop into a *horizontal* worker co-op. Then we brought in people who also carried these elements from their past experiences. It's taken almost six years to get to where we are; to flatten the wage, to create guidelines of power sharing and communication, to divide the work evenly and to change it when it's not working. There are actually very diverse opinions amongst us and we have a diverse workplace. If, in organizations, we consciously set out to use these principles in every decision process, in the way we engage, the way we share work and talk openly about power imbalances, we may not eliminate them, but can, at least reduce them—then we have a chance.

One of the things from my anarchist background is that we can maintain our collective autonomy and still work with varying communities without giving up our principles or values. We can have our separate groups that work towards common goals; I'm totally supportive of that. It's taken years to get here.

AG: Tell me about how these philosophies work at Ecology Action

sc: Understand that Ecology Action is a horizontal worker run cooperative. This means it's really important in the way we interact with each other. Our decisions aren't based on making the most profit for everything. We sell materials; that's what we do. Seventy percent of our business is selling materials, but it's not based on getting the most money for something. We try to find out what's the most ethical thing that we can do with it and make money with it. We don't want to make money on the backs of other people; we call it multiple bottom lines. We check to see how our interactions will affect others that are not externalities, as economists like to say, but real factors in dealing with economies. Recycling is a dirty business. We don't want to send materials to Asia to be sorted by children in the backwoods where it pollutes their rivers just so Americans can consume products mindlessly. For plastic to travel thousands of miles to be recycled doesn't make sense. We are always trying to find ways to deal with the waste stream products of capital that has the lowest impact.

Recycling, like voting, is not the answer. It's only degrees better than where we are now and something you should do if you don't do anything else. Pulling a lever, throwing paper into a bin is the least people can do, but it isn't going to make the changes we need. The house is on fire and we're still pissing on the fire instead of putting a hose to it. At Ecology Action we often tell people that recycling is not the answer. For us recycling is a way to talk to people about bigger issues like waste, not treating the earth as a resource, anarchy, collective decision making, etc. Then we start talking about other ways that people can make change—not personal choices, but working together for structural changes. We are shifting culture.

The way we work is important. Each staff person only works four days a week. Thirty two to thirty five hours is full time. We have full pay benefits—health care, dental, vision. We get a paid week long vacation every 10 weeks, it's called a furlough, because our job is so physically and administratively demanding. It gets to be stressful, so we put that in place for our health and well-being. We have sick leave. These are all things that we do on a $500,000 budget, as well as a flat wage. We keep the job sustainable as much as we can.

Ecology Action also does things outside of recycling that are important. Education on the one hand, but also supporting homeless people and street sex workers that have nothing to do with recycling, but are in proximity to our location. We treat those people with respect and dignity and allow the needle exchange and AIDS services to come and do their work.

At Treasure City and Ecology Action, we don't call the police unless there is absolutely no other choice. It's not the default if a situation is dangerous or escalates. We have a range—I'll call it a spectrum of violence because that's what it is. It starts with nonviolence on one end and violence on the other end—and the violence of calling the state is at the most extreme end. There's a spectrum of what tools people can chose to deal with these situations. It begins by using words, then may move to macing people to make them leave, to calling comrades for support, to defending yourself with a baseball bat if needed. But consciously choosing to de-escalate then move to threat of use of force, to use of force then as a last resort calling the police. The use of social justice elements give people more tools to bypass dealing with the state and reinforcing large social problems. It comes from a safety and self-defense stand point. Being a horizontal worker co-op has allowed us to incorporate social, political, economic, and environmental justice components that are important in creating new models for re-envisioning our world.

AG: Tell me about how these philosophies work at Treasure City Thrift.

sc: I'm just one of the co-founders. I wrote the plan for Treasure City Thrift in 2004, then went to New Orleans in '05 and again in '06. When I came back, I floated the idea with an initial group of people that met to talk about it, but that group fell apart. In 2006 another group formed, fourteen of us, that ended up co-founding and creating it. It is really a simple formula; take the thrift stores model that has been used for a long time to raise money for non-profits or church organizations. There's a long history of this—Salvation Army and Goodwill are the two best known.

We wanted to do one in Austin that would be local and give money to other anarchist and radical projects that can't get funding easily—as mentioned earlier, the Inside Books Project. To give money to give free books to prisoners is a hard sell. Indymedia and The Yellow Bike Project are others.

The idea had three elements: one, to get money in the hands of local organizations so they didn't have to spend time fund-raising. Another was to keep stuff out of the landfill by working with Ecology Action to collect, recycle, and reuse materials. The third component was to empower a horizontal worker co-op/volunteer collective based on Spanish anarchist models. The Spanish anarchists actually had some paid staff people but then they also had volunteers who worked too. Treasure City grew from those concepts. I think we started with $10,000 and we've been through 3 locations now. It's taken a few years—we've only had one paid staff person for a number of years, until last year. Treasure City started in 2006 and by 2012 it finally had four paid staff.

I left the collective officially in 2009 to work on other projects but I still volunteer from time to time. I'm not involved in the day-to-day. It has just exponentially grown from a grassroots, scrappy organization, really grown and still kept most of its liberatory roots. Again, it uses the same elements that were put in Common Ground and Ecology Action. Treasure City is more than just a worker co-op from the standpoint of economics, but because it is grounded in ideas of social justice.

AG: How does Treasure City Thrift serve its workers, the other worker collectives, and the communities in which it is located by integrating social, political, and cultural elements like the slogan, "solidarity not charity"?

SC: Well, at a fundamental level it creates a job with a living wage, a job with dignity and respect for the worker. It gives people an opportunity to practice participatory democracy in regular, day-to-day life. Those are the fundamentals. In a larger sense, the "solidarity not charity" is about recognizing that you're not just trying to alleviate problems of government and corporations and allow them to continue the corrupt economic and social paths that we're on. There is a desire to challenge those institutions and practices by doing something meaningfully different that will effect many in the creation of something else.

I think that Treasure City (TCT) strives to do that at some rudimentary levels. First, by creating these jobs, but also in the way they interact with the people that they serve. They work to serve communities that are marginalized in society like low income people, street sex workers, and homeless people. They offer more than just material goods like Goodwill or Salvation Army. By challenging social norms, power and oppression, they also recognize that there are multiple communities who they are tied up with. TCT also willingly breaks the law by allowing a free needle exchange a space to do outreach. That is technically illegal in this city. They also allow AIDS and social workers to come there and talk to people about HIV and distribute free condoms. Additionally they provide good, low-cost materials to people for whom those materials may be out of their economic reach. They provide free clothes to kids so they can get to school and have school supplies. They also give $20 vouchers to immigrants just released from Detention who live at Casa Marianella.

I think the larger piece is the idea of collective liberation, this social and political analysis, the creation of alternative economies that have multiple bottom lines. It's not just a business in a capitalist system, but it's a business that strives to create its own autonomy and yet be part of the fabric that is a weave of all the communities in Austin.

Although Treasure City and Ecology Actions are listed as non-profits, they both operate with the idea that we're not beholden to fund-raising. or foundations for support. We don't actively solicit donations; we generate our own funds. We will take donations, but if people give us money, they can't tell us what to do with it. This came from what was learned in the Common Ground Collective. We told people we are autonomous and will not be told how we may or may not use the money. I think that's critical.

It is a process of small steps to achieve these changes. The way I see it, you have to create a long-term vision, and then take steps to move toward. We know that we will fail at some levels but that's part of it. It is three steps forward, two steps back. Sometimes you get to a dead-end or see a split in the road and must choose another path you never even considered. It's like branches that grow, one from the other. Well, that's where we're at. We just take baby steps towards bigger changes.

AG: You mentioned that co-ops are not the answer, but steps towards something else. Why is that?

sc: I don't believe that worker co-ops are *the* answer of alternatives to capitalism. One of the things we say in our recycling work is that we'd love to work ourselves out of a job. The transformation of economies is something that we can't even think about right now. I want to be clear about that, that when I talk about worker co-ops, I see them in the short-term for the next 20 or 30 or 40 years as very viable things. But I don't see them supplanting and/or really transforming civil society. I would like to see 'work' as we know it disappear.

I don't believe all jobs are valuable or that every widget that some-body wants to make has intrinsic value. But we often treat 'jobs' and the economy like a cult religion, even among radicals. I have problems with that. That's one of the reasons I have issues with blind leftist support of unions without question. I don't think it is either healthy or revolutionary. I would rather see us put more energy into creating smaller worker co-ops rather than to democ-ratize shitty companies for a minority of workers. I don't want better Ford's or IBM's or Exxon's. I don't want those companies at all. Unions had an important place, but is it prudent to support them always, without question? My answer is no. I think horizon-tal worker co-ops offer a way out of the union hole for example. Everything produced does not have actual value. Look in any Walmart, shopping mall, or landfill.

Additionally most co-ops have a creeping liberalism to them. They may have started out with liberatory aspirations, but often have just become a subculture under capitalism. This would describe the first two collectives and co-ops I co-founded. The co-op move-ments are often white, middle class liberals on one hand or white liberals who support marginalized communities and build co-ops from within a nonprofit framework. Most co-ops are also siloed, meaning that they are just independent businesses focused on that only, instead of broader political movements. These are challenges co-ops face if they want to move out of the capitalist model.

AG: Before we end, do you have anything else you'd like to say that we haven't touched on?

sc: I think that worker co-ops show by example an alternative way to integrate your job with the rest of your life that is different than work at some large corporation. There it is part of your life because they're demanding 60 hours a week out of you. Your whole life revolves around that immersion which is likely disconnected from the rest of your life. Even If you don't care about the job, you tell yourself I'm going to make x amount of dollars or whatever.

Worker co-ops offer a space that integrates the social and cultural values that are beyond simple economic exchange. In a collective liberation frame, your work intersects with environmental and social issues that are not just related to the 'work' or money. My job isn't part of my life because I'm chasing money solely to live the rest of my life. I think it's important for it to be more than that otherwise we are still tools in the capitalist or whatever economies. To have dignity and respect at our workplace and that it culturally fits in without dominating our lives, are small steps in our liberation. I think that's an important piece of worker co-ops we don't usually talk about.

When I'm talking about these bigger ideas, that are not mine, understand that I have internalized them. For example, we must reduce our economies to scale and localize them into smaller components. We have to scale back the economies that we have. They are absolutely unsustainable at any level. We can't continue to treat the earth, nonhuman animals, and ourselves as infinite resources to burn up without consideration of the consequence. For example, we can't continue to ship produce 3,000 miles across the globe so wealthy people can have strawberries all year round. It is in no way sustainable; localized food production might be more sustainable. If we want people to leave the capitalist system then we need to show them something different. Communities need to control the means of local production, from growing food, to transporting it, to sale of food, to the care of the workers' children. These things should be integrated to benefit thousands of people in every bioregion.

We need to start thinking at a much more fundamental level about what can we can do to transform civil society and create new worlds that we hadn't even thought of yet, beyond capitalism, Power, civilization and work as we know them. I don't mean to have independent businesses based in the capitalist system. It is not about lessening the burden of living under unsustainable economic systems. In all of this I think that worker co-ops are incredibly viable alternatives with which to create these small localized alternative economies, even in the shorter term. I think it is also important to recognize that we're part of a long anarchist lineage. If we look to those histories, then we can build a more powerful future.

//

Anne M Gessler received her Ph.D. in the American Studies Department at The University of Texas at Austin with a focus on cooperative development.

Shifting Culture Without Government

By DJ Pangburn
Originally appeared: Medium; February 22, 2013

I recently spoke to noted anarchist community organizer scott crow about how average people—people with dreams, vision, grit and motivation—can effect change in a very real and quantifiable way after the vote. This isn't a playbook for smashing some McDonald's or Starbucks windows, but for taking the fight to communities.

A tired cycle exists in American electoral culture. Every two years we vote for federal representatives and senators, and every four years we vote in the presidential election. Each election cycle builds to a critical mass of ideological recriminations, crescendoing on election day.

Americans then rather sadly wash their hands of the mess, and resolve to do very little, or nothing, to actively make democracy work. There is a relinquishing of the responsibility of democracy to representatives. And as we've seen in the last twelve years of bitter partisan divide, it has produced paralysis instead of results. It has popularized politicians who behave more like actors or programmed holograms than actual problem solvers.

Mr. crow has had a roughly two decade-long resume of working in community organizing circles, most notably as one of the founders of the Common Ground Collective, one of the largest and most-organized volunteer forces in the post-Katrina wasteland. When W's buddy "Brownie" (Michael Brown) was botching the FEMA response, and the National Guard was enforcing martial law on New Orleans streets, CGC was busy cleaning out destroyed homes, mobilizing free health-care, clothing, and food, and otherwise delivering mutual aid to a grateful New Orleans population.

Much of crow's current work involves helping communities build worker cooperatives and local economies horizontally.

WE ARE MORE THAN JUST VOTERS & CONSUMERS

The voter, says crow, must pass into oblivion. In his or her place must arise the doer, the creator—that person who sees all potential and jumps into action.

Ancient Rome suffered a political paralysis similar to contemporary America. In Rome voters were mostly irrelevant. Into this political void came the Roman emperors who, while bringing some domestic stability, only hastened Rome's fall. Whereas the great American political paralysis might be a melancholic moment for this country's patriots, scott crow on the other hand sees vast opportunities to do great things.

"There are a set of paths in the middle that we haven't even explored to a great extent in this country," says crow. "The dominant paradigm tells us that we are just voters and consumers with a void of other alternatives. Life—politics, culture and economies—[involves] more complicated social relationships in this country."

The trick, says crow, is to be a creator: someone who sees new paths and pursues them energetically. "The [new paths] aren't always going to be easy," says crow. "But we will be doing them together; block by block and community by community, as needed."

Asked if voting has any real redeeming value, crow is mostly pessimistic. "Voting is a lot like recycling: if you're so damned lazy that you can't do anything else, then at least do that," says crow. "It's the least you can do. Pulling the lever or throwing something in the correct bin; neither require great effort or thinking, but neither have real impact either."

Community organizers like crow have no time for political saviors. They are individuals who eschew antiquated democratic politics, dreamers and doers who depart the political reservation for more unknown trajectories.

"We've had this mythology of the Great White Hope, that some great leader who will take us from our chains into the future," notes crow, a little astonished that so many still buy into the collective democratic hallucination. "When 'he' fails—as they always do—we blame the person and not the systems that got us there. We need to look anew at our world and think of the different ways we can engage with the world, our city, our neighborhoods, and ourselves."

"We have other choices," adds Crow. "Why is that we demand choices in MP3 players, sodas or schools for example but not in our economic, cultural or political systems that affect everything about us and our world?"

Issues Do Not Exist in Isolation

Americans have the tendency to engage issues in isolation. For the extreme (and even the mainstream) conservatives, "socialism," "immigrants" or "gays" are the viruses corrupting the system—other domestic and international considerations be damned. A matrix of interrelated issues work at one another like a neural network. One cause may have several effects. And that cause may itself be the byproduct of other variables.

"If you want to stop hunger, you can't just go, Well, I'll just feed somebody and it's over," says crow. "You start with that and then ask, Why are they hungry? Did they not have access to good schooling? So then we need to fix the schools or create new ones. Did they not have good access to jobs? Then we need to create good jobs with a living wage, dignity, and respect. Or did they have health care issues that aren't being addressed, even just basic stuff? Well then we need to get community clinics in every community so that people can have their basic needs looked at before they become major issues like cancer or diabetes."

Crow had to look toward more revolutionary movements for this sort of education.

"I had to look at what the Black Panthers and the Zapatistas did for their communities," says crow. "I had to look at what the Spanish anarchists did when fascism was taking over. They were inspiring in that they helped their people and rebuilt their world. Those are just political references. In every subculture, whether it's religious groups, charities, or hip-hop communities, there are examples of people doing things themselves without waiting for government or other people to do it."

"In what I like to call 'anarchism with a little 'a', we need to explore ideas of direct action so that we're not waiting on others to fix the problems," adds crow. "We will do it ourselves. Mutual aid, cooperation, collective liberation—the idea that we're all in this together. But there also needs to be an awareness that you are in this yourself."

Crow points out the unvarnished political reality: no leader, party or group is going to do this for Americans. But there is a more salient point. Even if a single leader or political party had this sort of desire, the country is far too big and complex for such national policymaking. They are mere band-aids on gushing wounds.

"We need to de-centralize and localize to solve the problems around us, while looking to support other communities doing the similar things and connect on larger issues," says crow. "And to do this we have to first look at history."

CREATE LOCALIZED ECONOMIES

"It's absolutely cliché to say we need to think globally and act locally," says crow. "But that's exactly what we need to do while we are creating localized economies (gift, barter, or local currencies), opening the common spaces from the holds of corporate private property (like shopping malls) and becoming neighbors again."

"We need to know what is happening around the world and share the information, successes and challenges that we face in our communities to help each other," adds crow. "What happens to a rice farmer in India or a landless peasant in Brazil or a family in Appalchia is of utmost importance to me in thinking of supporting each other. The internet and social media in particular will help in this flow of information."

Perhaps the most important lesson in the recent trend of localization is that scaling down just might be what saves us. It doesn't require a singular savior but hundreds of millions, indeed billions of them. Centralized government and corporations haven't worked for humanity, argues crow. And who would disagree in this second decade of the 21st century?

"Centralizing corporations—these giant pyramids with elites at the top—aren't working out for the rest of us," adds crow. "And it's not just the 99%—it's not working out for any of us, not even some of the elites."

Government and industry aren't the only institutions ripe for a downsizing, according to crow—the world's social movements could use it as well. "Instead of having one big movement, what if we have thousands of decentralized movements that are working toward common ideals?" suggests crow. "We need to value difference."

In crow's practical wisdom this means not one ideological boat but many boats full of a multitude of dreams and ideas. "We start to move at our own pace," foresees crow. "And we help each other along but maintain our autonomy and differences as individuals, neighborhoods, communities, etc., at the same time cooperating when necessary to reach the goals."

Organizers like crow have noticed that even corporations are starting to see things this way. "Instead of trying to centralize, they're breaking it down," says crow. "They see networks having advantages over their traditional hierarchies. Advertising is doing this in the corporate world in what they call micro-marketing."

Crow also wants people to stop confusing convenience and choices with democracy. This is a difficult proposition in America, a country that has trained its citizens from an early age to expect convenience. And what is voting if not the culmination of convenience culture and democracy?

"A choice of 50 different soft drinks doesn't make us any more democratic than any other country," says crow. "Especially when those 50 soft drinks are made by five or ten companies. The same could be extrapolated to political parties. There's a perception of choice, but it's not meaningful or real and definitely not democratic."

Build Horizontally

The worker cooperative has certainly entered the popular American lexicon, but it wasn't always so. Intrigued early on by the co-op's possibilities, crow says resources and literature on the subject were sparse. So he and other Austin organizers educated themselves and just started building their own. Eventually it led to horizontalization: the process of co-ops and other services overlapping in communities. Crow has spent the last several years building horizontal worker cooperatives and consulting when he can.

"There's no boss and everyone involved makes the same wage and has the same amount of say in their futures," says crow. "I'm interested in creating localized jobs for people with dignity, respect, and a living wage. These businesses have the potential to be small scale economic engines for localized economies, where we start to close the loop in taking care of our own transportation, health-care, cultural, and educational centers in neighborhoods or communities."

Crow envisions a community in which these services would be offered to anybody who needs them. "These services would be offered in various neighborhoods and they would start to overlap," says crow, with an enthusiasm that is contagious. "Imagine instead of big box stores taking up acres of land, there were farm stands, free health clinics, or small functioning schools on every corner. Community members of all stripes could actually benefit instead of corporations and governments sucking the resources away."

EMPOWER THE DISEMPOWERED

A certain percentage of the US population believes that the poor and disempowered can only be lifted up through tax breaks and the good auspices of job creators. While job creation has its economic and political benefits (cynically, employed populations are much more passive than its opposite), it often doesn't empower any individuals in the labor force. There is the perception of power: a wage pays the rent and all of life's necessities. Beyond that, is there any substantial and meaningful empowerment?

"At Ecology Action [a recycling co-op] we often supported the homeless people that surrounded us," says crow. "First by not criminalizing them but treating them with dignity and respect, then by allowing other service organizations to provide services like HIV information and testing, a needle exchange (which is illegal in Austin). Third we also provided a downtown space where people could sleep after hours as long as they followed guidelines we set up with them."

Ecology Action, as crow notes, also held meetings with the transient population and made them reinforce the guidelines amongst themselves. "We never called the cops unless severe violence was taking place," says crow.

Crow remembers one man's empowerment in particular. "There was this one guy who just had a streak of bad luck, who didn't have a drug or alcohol problem, and he lived on our lot for a year and volunteered," remembers crow. "We ended up hiring him in and he worked for Ecology Action for almost 3 ½ years. His experience as a 55 year old black man, who had never heard of horizontal organizing but worked at a job where his voice counted was an eye-opening, transformational experience for all of us. When he left he said it was the best job he had ever had.

"It didn't make us saints or saviors," says crow. "But it was a small piece of what we could do. And it's not the only example."

Crow points to the Occupy movement when speaking of power sharing. "It was the first grassroots movement of movements in this country, very decentralized," says crow. "I went to 24 different Occupy camps across the country last year and all of them looked very different. "But there were very similar elements to them: the ideas of participatory democracy, power sharing amongst the people, the use of affinity groups, mic checks, general assemblies and spokes council models, etc. All of those things came out of at least 20 years of anarchism and decentralized organizing in this country."

Community organizers like crow also see small businesses as integral to real empowerment. "The real engines of this country are small business," says crow. "Corporations have more concentrated wealth, but there are still more small businesses employing more people everywhere. Some small businesses are starting to make themselves more egalitarian."

Crow sees a trend of sharing power and resources because it makes sense. But he's quick to point out that this is not just his myopic view. "It's happening all over the world," says crow, thrilled by this subtle cultural revolution. "And it's happening not because of one voice but many voices.

"There's more worker cooperatives, more intentional communities, consumer cooperatives, agricultural cooperatives than ever before. They're on the rise. And what's beautiful about it is that nothing is driving it but need and necessity."

SHIFT CULTURE, BE AN INNOVATOR

Boring, informational leaflets aren't just going to cut it any longer, says crow. Not when corporate media can tailor its advertising message to individual subcultures in communities.

"If we don't create our own counter-advertising, we're just shooting ourselves in the foot," says crow. "Living in this present political and economic system, we must use its tools. Creating beautiful posters, books, social/web media and videos."

There is no better advertising than creating something better, says crow. People often need "to be shown by example what it can look like," says crow. "Make it appeal it to people. Traditional advertising is part of that. Crimethinc has been doing it for 10 years. Just Seeds Artist Cooperative and Little Black Cart press are some other groups that have developed aesthetics with knowledge."

"Our roles as radicals of all kinds, activists and organizers is to move ideas from the margin to the mainstream—that's really what we do," says crow, who reminds us that slavery was at one point culturally and economically embedded in America's DNA. "We would not have built this country the way we did without slavery," says crow. "Working to abolish slavery was an act of sedition—a crazy, radical idea." This type of cultural shift, says crow, is what is needed in America.

"We need to stop protesting and think of other ways of doing things like creative interventions and valuing aesthetics along the way," says crow.

No Government Required

It's almost a cliché to say that it only takes a small group of people to make change in this world. But it is a cliché that crow believes in wholeheartedly.

"After Hurricane Katrina, Common Ground Collective (CGC) was one organization of many that was doing things. At the most, we had 28,000 people involved from 2005 to 2008," says crow. "In that time we served over 150,000 families. It had a huge political, social, and cultural impact not only on New Orleans but on grassroots organizations around the United States." The life-transforming experiences of so many CGC volunteers reverberated.

"Many Occupy participants and organizers came through it," says crow. "CGC volunteers also went to Haiti as first responders. On the East Coast, Occupy Sandy and other decentralized grassroots efforts have taken CGC's models in new directions. Occupy Sandy organizers reached out directly to some of the core CGC organizers who either went and put boots on the ground or consulted."

Crow believes that people have more power than they can imagine.

"Change is scalable," says crow. "It doesn't take much for ideas to spread. Look at all the bad ideas governments and corporations have spread over the decades. Remember Crystal Pepsi or the War on Iraq?"

EXPERIENCE MORE & BE CONTENT NOT KNOWING THE ANSWERS

Not knowing all of the answers doesn't bother crow at all. He believes an anarchist, community organizer, or cultural innovator should be prepared to learn. Lack of answers can function as the seeds for new ideas.

"I learned from the Zapatista Revolution that as revolutionaries you don't have to have the answers, just be willing to look at and be open to possibilities," says crow, who believes the old days of "1-2-3- steps to revolution" failed and are now dead.

"My other role as an organizer—and part time futurist—is to be an innovator to challenge our own radical assumptions and ways of engaging as well as envisioning and spreading new ideas or ways to engage," adds crow.

"I do this because I love people and have seen for decades that we have the creativity—once we add the determination and willingness to make substantial and powerful changes, we do," concludes crow, ever hopeful against the prospect of the unknown.

"We are always standing on the edge of potential—so how is it going to look?"

//

DJ Pangburn is editor-in-chief of Konbini and contributor to VICE, Boing Boing, Medium. Motherboard, OMNI Reboot, MTV, Death and Taxes and, Makeshift. He is also a filmmaker and Pataphysician.

How I Learned to Not Care About Winning Over Cops to Join Occupy Wall Street

By Nathan Diebenow
Originally appeared: Diebenow.org; September 28, 2011

It's not everyday that you get to hang out with someone who toured with Nine Inch Nails, co-organized the largest anarchist-influenced organization in modern American history, or whom the FBI labeled a "domestic terrorist." I had the opportunity to interact with all three of these 'someones' in the form of one scott crow.

You might have heard of the FBI's shenanigans against crow and his friends from the New York Times, Democracy Now, or from Rag Radio, but if you haven't heard it, I highly recommend his Rag Radio interviews not only because crow speaks more on alternative economic systems but also because played are clips of the political industrial dance music he co-created with his former group Lesson Seven in Dallas in the late '80s and early '90s.

Had you sat in on crow's talk at Occupy Denton, you would have received a more in-depth look at the last 25 years of his experiences organizing communities—such as those at the University of North Texas (UNT) in the anti-apartheid movement in 1985 to those in New Orleans days after Hurricane Katrina threw the gross racial and wealth inequalities of the region in the face of the One Percent.

Because of the horrific police actions against Occupy Oakland when veteran Scott Olson received serious brain injuries on Oct. 25 2011 following a general feeling among some occupiers that the cops are also part of the 99 Percent, I intended to speak with crow about the Occupy movement's relation to the State. Thankfully, he also occupied the conversation toward the nature of social movements and the history of previous organizing efforts that led to the Occupy movement's structure.

Here is the fruit of our discussion after his talk at Occupy Denton on the UNT campus off Fry Street, tents and all:

Nathan Diebenow: What do you think about the "Occupy Police" wing of Occupy movement on Facebook and Twitter? Are you skeptical about the solidarity that this group espouses? Or are you hopeful that it will break the bubble that surrounds the police?

scott crow: I'm absolutely skeptical of that because one, the Occupy movement is super decentralized. There's no one voice in that. Anybody who purports to speak for all the Occupy movements going on is total bullshit. Secondly, I think one of the things we have to realize in this country is that the police, like a lot of wealthy people who may be interested in what's going on, are never going to join these movements until it effects them directly. People in upper middle class strata, like very upper middle class strata at the top of the 99 Percent who feel like they don't feel a part of it, and the police, until it effects their bottom line, until the banks are closed, until the ATMs are not working, until their checks aren't coming, their pensions are gone, then they will join the movement. But the police are never going to side with us until that happens. The police are paid to uphold private property of corporations, corporations, and the state. That's their job. I mean, that's their mandate. Given the order to shoot me, they're going to do it. Is that dramatic enough? [laughs] But it's true.

ND: What you just described to me is basically like if you see any of those things happening, you'll be less skeptical. I mean, we're talking system-wide.

sc: There are individual good cops. I'm not going to lie. I mean, I've dealt with lots of them over the years, but I know ultimately their job—what they get paid for day-in and day-out—is to uphold the state. They have loyalty to that whether they want to or not. They have families to feed. They're on a hamster wheel, and they're spinning in that. They are part of the system as much as anybody is. They're not separate from that, and they have to make moral decisions based on that. So maybe that won't shoot me dead, but they might tear gas the hell out of me to make me stop what I'm doing if it's against their interests.

ND: And that played out yesterday in Oakland. Even with the supposed "non-violent" weapon like rubber bullets.

sc: It's less lethal. I mean, but let's be clear about it. Rubber bullets are *less* lethal. They're not non-lethal. I know people who have been incredibly injured by them.

ND: So in the way it's playing out right now nationwide, it's kind of as you'd expect it in terms of the reaction of the state with the Occupy movement.

sc: Let's really talk about what's important about the Occupy movement. You're talking about a movement that hasn't happened in the United States in a long time—a decentralized movement not controlled by any central organization or anything, where people rose up because things were wrong all over. The Tea Party, which was a similar thing on the right-leaning spectrum, was always geared toward funneling people into the Republican Party, or it was quickly co-opted by people that had interest in doing it, like Dick Armey who used to be at the University of North Texas here.

But the Occupy movements are totally decentralized. It's 30 years of anarchist and horizontal organizing coming to fruition, where you talk about General Assembly, where you talk about consensus decisions, where you try to hear the voices of the people who aren't normally heard. Are there problems within that? Yeah, but that's an amazing start for something. All the Occupy movements—nobody is going around saying, "Hey, you should start an occupy movement. You should start an occupy movement." People are doing it because they have the sense of need to do that. That is what we should be talking about. Not the state repression. Fuck the state. If we stay clear on what we are doing, it doesn't matter what the state does. Do you know what I mean? Our will—our political will is much stronger than anything they can throw at us. They don't call it struggle for nothing, right? But we stay focused on what we're doing, and it doesn't matter what they do.

ND: In your talk I liked your point about the terms long-term revolution and little revolutions. It's almost like little struggles.

sc: They are. With every large rupture that occurs in social movements, there were smaller ruptures that came before and lulls in between. Lulls meaning times of healing and reflection—not that nothing is happening.

ND: So this is a big revolution in the sense that it was long time coming, but it is still in a sense little revolutions for individuals.

sc: It is baby steps. Every movement that rises up, like the alternative globalization movement that I was talking about that was a decade ago, it's the same thing. But what happens is that we have

no institutional memory because we don't carry it from movement to movement. So the hundreds of thousands of people that
were in the alternative globalization movement left, and there's
only a few of us left, and we're the ones who tell the stories so that
the new people who are rising up can (learn), and in 10 years,
these people can tell the stories.

**ND: I was listening to Amy Goodman talk the other night,
and she was saying how she studies movements. And what
was interesting was when you said you studied revolutions.
Is there a difference?**

sc: Revolutions are the idea that we have to overturn all of these
things to make things happen. Movements are what rise up when
we try to make these revolutionary situations, and the things that
come out of them. I'm not talking old school like we're going to rise
up one day, fight and then we take state power. That's not the kind
of revolutions I'm talking about. Actually, I don't even know what
they can look like. They're going to move faster in some areas and
slower in other areas, but the little mini-revolutions are happening daily. First it's the wakening of each and every one of us, and
then us pulling together and doing things, and then inheriting the
other movements that came before us, and then building on those
futures, which we don't even know what they're going to be yet.
And I'm okay with that. I used to not because I wanted a plotted
out plan: "We're going to do this, this and this. And then next thing
there is, we're all free." But that's not going to happen.

But what's different with the Occupy movement is that nobody
wants to control anything. The Tea Party wanted to control things.
I don't want to hit them with a broad stroke because I think that's
unfair, too, because there are a lot of legitimate people within the
Tea Party movement, and there was a huge spectrum of interest
within that, right? But ultimately when they got funneled in, they

wanted to control what happened in the new store. We don't want to control that. We want to create new worlds from below and from the left that we don't even know what they are. We're imagining something different, and people are waking up and trying to re-imagine what those worlds are. We've all been in these cages that we can't see, and people are waking up, starting to go, "Wow. I'm not in that cage, but what is it like to be free? I knew what I could do inside the cage, but now I have to figure out..." And those paths are much harder. That's where I come to that thing "walking and asking." So you continue to ask questions along the way. And the thing is, these are the modern revolutions. The Zapatistas set that up, where you didn't have to have the answers because we don't have the answers, and that makes us have fallible but human revolutions on a global scale.

ND: One final thought: the Occupy movement has created an alternative government.

SC: If you think about it, the Occupy movement in city after city, they are practicing democracy—direct democracy—not where you're voting your life away for somebody 3,000 miles away from you who is going to tell you what to do. You're actually practicing it. And that takes a lot of time. We've been resisting for so long, and we need to build. Our resistance arm is totally muscular and really strong, but our building arm is totally atrophied because we've ignored it. Now we're beginning to practice building it. It is like alternative governments and alternative societies. We have to re-imagine it. It's baby steps. Just because not everybody is on board with some clear agenda is beautiful to me because it shows the openness and the willingness to really think about it and let it stew. In all the movements like in Argentina and what rose up in Chiapas, Mexico, that's what's happened with people. The uprising in Chiapas, Mexico, in 1994 was 20 years in the making. Twenty years they talked about it before they decided to do that.

ND: In a wider sense, is this like an Abraham Lincoln Brigade? Is that movement part of this movement's history as well?

sc: You're talking the Spanish Civil War. That's a totally different thing. That was a clear enemy. They were fighting against fascism and for anarchism and socialism. This is way different than that. I wouldn't compare it to that at all. I would compare it to Argentina in 2000, and before that, I would compare it to Central American movements in the 1970s. It's people's uprisings. The thing is, there's no leaders telling people they should rise up. There's no Communist Party or Socialist Party. And everybody doesn't want a socialist state. That's not what I want. I'm not trying to build a socialist state, I want to abolish the state. I want us to build grassroots power. I want to take the longest, hardest path that we can find to figure out what it's going to be. I don't want an easy answer because easy answers end up with dictators and fascists.

//

Nathan Diebenow is a recovering poet and accidental journalist.

When It's Broken:
On Accountability and Alternatives to the Police

By Debbie Russell and scott crow
Peaceful Streets Project Summit presentation; July 14, 2012

Editors Note: This is a re-worked version from an excerpted talk at the first national conference of the Peaceful Streets Project, a police accountability and alternatives group founded in Austin Texas, which was held in a bingo hall in East Austin.[1] This is a co-presentation from Debbie Russell, long time community organizer and ACLU board member and scott crow. Debbie mostly addresses current accountability and reforms available while scott mostly addresses alternatives to policing and the criminal justice systems.

Debbie Russell: I'm Debbie Russell, community organizer. I'm glad to be the first woman speaking at the Peaceful Streets event so far!

Audience: [laughter/applause]

scott crow: And my name is scott crow and I'm an anarchist community organizer.

The reason that y'all are here and that we've come together is that some want justice in these systems while others of us want to take our communities back. We want to stop this systemic racism. We want to stop this systemic injustice. These are our neighborhoods; they're our family members. We know these people who are being

1   For more about Peaceful Streets see their site: http://peacefulstreets.com/

brutalized, imprisoned, and killed. We need to hold the police accountable on one hand, but we also want to create power from below by getting rid of the police and criminal injustice systems. Do you agree with that?

Audience: Yes!

sc: Some of my part of this talk comes out of my experiences dealing with the police and courts in my life and as an activist for over twenty five years, having been targeted by the FBI for a decade for political activities and my experiences after Hurricane Katrina where some of us, black and white, took up arms against the police and white vigilantes to stop the racist killings that were happening in solidarity with largely black communities who were being targeted. Those actions of armed community self-defense were about more than just guns, guts, and glory; they were part of the larger hard work of building autonomous community alternatives outside state control. Because solving the problem with police is not just about the police themselves. It's so much more. We have to create localized social safety nets without governments to create power from below. We need health care, education, drug and alcohol counseling, jobs with dignity—all of these pieces can help to rebuild atomized and fractured communities to mediate problems that we have outside of institutions—especially the police and the courts.

DR: There's a lot to say about the problems with policing, we're going to talk briefly about some of them. Then go into reforming the policing systems today, as well as alternatives to these systems. So, we're going to ask a question here. Why do people need the police?

Audience: (summary) To mediate conflict! For our protection! To right a wrong been done against you!

DR: How do they do in those three areas?

Audience: Terrible!

sc: We agree that there's systemic problems with the police. I just want to say I don't want to reform the police. I want us to abolish the police; and to do that it's going to take all kinds of tools and tactics—and all of us.

Let's talk about the police as mediators. Who has had a bad interaction with the police where they've mediated conflict? A lot of us. They're terribly trained in conflict mediation in most situations. They often end up arresting both parties as default, or using excessive force against people to assert control of the situation. The police are often out of their element in dealing with issues of domestic violence, drug and alcohol problems, or mental health issues due to bad training, inherent biases around racism, or enforcing bureaucratic laws. But many people call them anyway because they have guns and the backing of the state to use force we would get in trouble using.

Someone mentioned protection. So who are the police protecting? They have always been an occupying force from their beginnings that have historically sided with the property owners and business. As overseers of the plantations first doing the work of the slave masters, then as private security for the political machines in cities, and today the police overseers still predominantly protect the wealthy and property. How many rich people do you see in prison? Not many. Leaving the rest of us to fend for ourselves—or against them, especially if you're poor or a person of color.

One of their original roles as 'public servants' was to protect people from being hurt by violent crime, like being robbed or mugged with nightsticks or guns. Then along the way governments and military contractors hyper militarized the police, first under the 'war on drugs', then later under the 'war on terror'. The specialized SWAT team became standard issue. You see all those high-tech military toys that they love to get. That's helicopters, computers, battering rams; all these gadgets. But our streets aren't safer; they're actually more destructive than they were before through sanctioned legal use of force. Just ask anyone from a marginalized community. Think about this, their jobs entails killing people over property—minor theft, non-violent break-ins, stolen goods. They too often shoot people for this.

What is the Austin city bloated budget for police?

DR: Actually, the public safety budget is about 65 percent the general fund, with the police receiving the majority of it—over schools, public safety (*ed. which includes fire and paramedics*) and infrastructure maintenance or repair.[2]

And, in terms of the militarization, we have seen a lot of movement in recent years. The federal funding from various programs, like Secure Communities, which targets undocumented immigrants, Homeland Security, which targets Muslims and political activists, and gang containment, which mostly targets youth of color, are all driving the police departments to criminalize huge segments of the population. Additionally departments adhere to a certain standard of military training and cohesiveness amongst forces at city, county, state, and federal levels. That model has been adopted in every police department around the country, so that they're prepared whenever there's another protest, 'terrorist attack', immigrant detention or 'gang' activity in their city. The federal dollars have attached to it things that they have to abide by, which they are incorporating for everyday use against communities.

sc: The last big issue mentioned was 'to right a wrong been done against you' through the establishment of laws and courts that are supposed to be fair to everyone. But because there's systemic in-

---

2   This percentage of funding for public 'safety' is about average for most of the larger cities in the US

stitutionalized racism in the police departments, and the injustice systems in general, there's no way that marginalized communities can ever get fairness in this system. If you're a poor person of color it's against you from the beginning. I know I'm preaching to the choir on this.

The second strand that really is important to remember is that the injustice system has grown so loaded and bureaucratic that it's completely out of touch with reality. Out of date 18th century laws based on the maxim "laws are of government and not of men" is out of control. Governments have made more complicated laws with complicated interpretations to criminalize more people for more things in the last 35 years than ever. All the while the police still get away with brutality and murders daily by bending those laws or being exempt from them.

DR: Just as an example of this, I was going to offer an analysis from the widely read *Grits for Breakfast* blog covers Texas laws and legislation.[3] There's 11 felonious laws about oysters, oyster collection, and oyster shells in Texas alone—out of our 2,600 sum-odd felonies in Texas.

Audience: [laughter]

sc: Let's talk about the laws really quickly. My analysis is that all laws are reactionary, arbitrary, bureaucratic, and selectively enforced. More often they are made too late and do too little to correct the problem they were written for, just look at any civil rights legislation for example; they all too often end up being used to criminalize people, whole communities, or activities outside of the intended law.

And laws are written by mostly white men who seem to exempt themselves and their buddies in the process.

3   http://gritsforbreakfast.blogspot.com/

We don't need all these laws. They don't always make us any safer. They don't make civil society more ordered. What they do is create specialized bureaucracies and hierarchies, where there's more courts, more judges, and more cops. The more laws the more the state enlarges itself.

It almost seems like the problems haven't changed despite 35 years of police oversight by governments or the public. And I think we all would agree, that lynching is still going on in this country, now it's just often extra-judicial. As Rene Valdez of Resistencia Books mentioned, they just can't posse up and take people out anymore, but what they can do is use lethal force on those in marginalized communities. Cops walk free after killing or brutalizing people everyday.

DR: Let's talk about some reforms available. We've done a lot of police accountability work in this town, people before me, and the people before those folks. A lot of fighting the racism that's inherent, a lot of trying to reform these systems. Many cities have Police Monitor's Office, which is attached to the Civilian Review Panel, where volunteers from the community act as liaisons to listen to complaints against the police and make judgments on them. But in most places all they can do is make recommendations.

The problem with the structure is contracts between the police union and city management. And so, when these two get together, usually behind closed doors, to make the final decisions, we get left out. In Austin recently we had a two-year-long Citizen Task Force to design a really good system to call the police's use of force into question, all of that got watered down behind those closed doors.

That is an apparent example of the injustice of our system. But back to the police monitor. You can make a complaint; it's not really going to go anywhere. But what it does do is create a record of it later. We can start to track some of these bad cops, look at the worst ones, and try to satisfy the community with what we're going to do about that.

I have done a lot of work with the community about police accountability over the years. We've raised a lot of issues. Lately, the most recent thing is the 'preservation of life standard'. What we did was raise the questions and concerns that property has been held at least as high as the value they place on life in police use of force. We saw a gentleman get killed, just a month ago, in his car, just driving home from work, because the cop decided that he had to high-speed chase an individual that he thought had stolen a car from a mall. We have laws in this country and policies that are better than that. We want to make sure that we can get that here, if we're talking about working from a reform standpoint, that they don't put people's property over people's lives. Because people are dying and it's atrocious.

So, the police and city put in what they call the 'preservation of life standard'. It is about a quarter of what we need from a legal standpoint to really have that in place. We're going to continue to work on that and I hope that's something y'all will join the police accountability folks in.

So, that's about it on that. We can go to the next part. We're going to talk about alternatives.

When you think about it, everybody probably knows a story where they called the police and things got worse. Somebody went to jail that shouldn't have. Somebody got hurt that shouldn't have. The whole thing was amplified and could have been handled better another way. It's just that we don't readily know what those *other ways* are.

sc: If we don't call the cops then what can we do? We want to challenge all of us to think before we call the police. So we're going to talk about the ideas of alternatives to calling the cops and means of building alternative futures that we might try, as well as some challenges we will face making those choices. When we're talking about taking control, we're not talking about George Zimmerman bullshit vigilante style. We're talking about using tools along with a power/privilege analysis so we can resolve conflicts amongst ourselves and others without calling the police. We're only going to scratch the surface in the time we have without going into detail about all of them, because each of these topics are in-depth.

An example is that I work at an anarchist work-run recycling center called Ecology Action and I co-founded an anarchist worker cooperative thrift store called Treasure City Thrift. Both are around downtown areas that deal with the general public. There's no bosses; all of us make decisions together. One of the decisions that we decided, as anarchists, was that we would *not* call the police at either place unless we were desperate from some situation.

Instead of continuing down that path when there were issues with people that ended with them in handcuffs or jail, which to us was a form of state sanctioned violence, we started to develop internal guidelines and tools. We called it a *spectrum of self-defense* we could use instead of calling the police.

We agreed unless something violently egregious happened or if people stole items from us, we would handle it outside the law, including banishing them from our spaces and letting people around them know. Property wasn't worth people's lives, violence, or the state.

We exercised our own power, critical thinking, experiences, and levels of safety in choosing our own escalating use of force, instead of just using force, which is what the police are going to do. Some of the tools that we use reduce the risk of violence. For example, if you need to make somebody leave. First, we have a conversation with them to ask them to leave where we stand firm, but quietly let them keep their dignity by not turning it into a public show. If that doesn't work then we may raise our voice or shout at them using a loud clear voice without condescension. The next escalation would be to posse up with two or three people from the collectives who are on the shift, standing kind of shoulder-to-shoulder and walking the person off the property; forcefully, but calm.

We also have tools for protection too, like pepper spray, an axe handle, or you could punch them too if you felt unsafe or were protecting yourself. And these are all are escalating tactics to minimize our use of violence, including power. And I can tell you that 99 percent of the time that we've had to deal with issues, it's been just using our voices to make people leave, or physically walking people off the lot or the store that worked the best repeatedly. It's amazing how just our willingness to handle it ourselves changes the dynamics in letting everyone keep their dignity and resolve situations.

In the six years I've was part of both of those collectives, I physically had to resort to violence twice out of over at least a hundred situations, from drunks to petty theft, to threats of violence from other. These tactics aren't always easy or hunky dory, but can be fairly successful. And how many times have we called the cops? At Ecology Action one time in six years—and we didn't want to, but the person was out of control physically where we all felt unsafe. We have called the paramedics quite a few times for emergency situations when people seemed liked they were going to harm themselves accidentally or on purpose. We also have used the *threat of use of force* often, meaning we made escalating threats.

These were collective actions of combinations of women, men, and trans people working together in these situations. It wasn't just a macho-fest.

Like I mentioned earlier both of these projects are in areas of high concentrations of homelessness and street sex workers. As many of you may know there is a lot of drug and alcohol abuse, mental health issues, and occasionally violence among these communities who are often the most marginalized and criminalized in most cities, with little support services or places to go, and no safety nets at all. We don't criminalize the homeless for being homeless. None of us should. We all know that many things poor people are criminalized for being on the edge with 'nuisance' laws like code violations, sleeping on the street, drinking or using drugs in public where its off limits, etc. Stuff we didn't care about unless it effected us.

Knowing this, we created a safe zone and we have tried to provide social services with limited ability, like a clean needle exchange and HIV services, and we built relationships with the people who were around us, the regulars if you will, which lead to some self-policing from some of those regulars and protection for us. At heart we're just a recycling center and thrift store using liberatory analysis, and we are respectful of the people who come around regardless of their economic situation or social status. We treat them with respect if they do the same. And if it goes awry, then we have a spectrum of tools to use instead of the police in those situations.

In choosing to take care of situations ourselves we recognized early on two important scenarios that we weren't able to deal with very well because it was beyond our limited capacity of resources or beyond our skill sets: when people had severe mental issues, or people are out of their head on drugs or alcohol. I am talking about people who are actively having violent psychotic episodes or so messed up on drug they can't see straight and are violent. You can't be rational with them in any form. Both of those situations were more likely to force us to bring in outside involvement, like paramedics.

DR: A cop is a force that should be used rarely, but it is a tool.

sc: In my own life, I never call the cops unless I'm absolutely desperate. I just don't. They've tried to kill me in the past, and I have lots of friends and family who've been imprisoned because of them. I will try to resolve the situation myself or with help first.

If it's a dispute with my neighbor, I will talk to them first. Remember, we often call the cops a lot of times because we're afraid we'll have conflict. If we don't want this police entity, we have to learn that conflict is part of self determination, and it's a lot more difficult to do.

DR: Yeah. Get your neighbors' phone numbers. If the music's too loud, call them, don't call the cops. It will just makes things worse. I am part of a local community related to the Burning Man Festival. Our regional festival is called Burning FlipSide; we have organized ourselves in this fashion. We have what are called Rangers. Rangers have power given to us by the community and we have to be accountable to our fellow burners to take care of safety and conflict both at the events and in our communities. We are volunteer participants in this community who choose to actually just walk around and make sure everything's OK while the event is going and beyond that we agreed to help with issues in our community. Conflict aren't always limited to the event space itself, so we apply these ideas and skills in our day-to-day lives. I've trained Rangers in conflict mediation and conflict resolutions skills.

As an example, if somebody sneaks into the event, causing a lot of problems, or putting people in danger, allegations of sexual assault or being sexually improper, when you're talking about large fires and people blowing things up, and things like that. And nobody feels threatened by us just because we're there, because we're not there with our mirrored sunglasses on and our weapons and being intimidating. We escort them off the property, try to get a hold of a family member. We'll utilize the resources we have, the property owners who know who the neighbors are and whose kid this might be. We're certainly not going to put this kid into the criminal justice system because he's trying to break into a party. I mean, come on, this is ridiculous.

We have had to call Emergency Medical Services a few times, and maybe the sheriff's department a couple of times out of over 12 years of running this event—but that is as a last resort. We deal with it, time and again, within our community.

We have to remember the level at which the conflict is and that we have tools to deal with that up until a certain point. So, we're going to be organized and prepared. Before we just deal with that, we need to talk with our neighbors and the community, and whatever associations or organizations were involved, and have these plans in place, and have some policies and guidelines so we're all on the same page. That's the most important part before you move forward and try to create a barrier between yourselves and the police and a criminal justice system that always makes things worse.

sc: We need to also recognize that systemic racism is alive and well. When communities start to take back control of themselves, especially largely white and largely middle class communities with some amounts of privilege or power, we have to be very aware of it. Don't feel guilty about having a little of either, just recognize that you have it, and that all communities are not the same. We need to recognize that each community is different, and each individual is different. If you have power/privilege use it to support communities that don't so they can build their own in solidarity, because our struggles our tied together. That's a start to seeing people and ourselves differently and to equalizing the discrepancies caused under these unequal systems.

DR: We're going to touch on a few other community tools really quickly, and then alternative justice.

sc: One of the really powerful things that comes and goes, are community patrols and neighborhood watches. When I talk about a neighborhood watch, I'm not talking about stupid *weed and seed* programs or *neighborhood watch* programs as you see them now, with the little signs telling people to call the cops at every turn and criminalize the poor, homeless, or street sex workers. I'm talking about neighborhood watches where people in the neighborhood get together and say, 'we're going to watch our neighborhood and take care of each other'. Ideally this wouldn't be a self-selected group of people but would be everyone involved at some level who are accountable to each other; to their sisters, to their brothers, to the children, to the grandmothers, and people who are around them and who can be called on for that. Neighborhood groups are very powerful sources to stop having to call the cops, resolving our own conflicts and for reconnecting neighbors to each other. Why? Because we begin to know each other and have relationships with each other built on trust and collective engagement. It's important to know that.

DR: And in that scenario we all have guidelines of respect, engagement, and accountability that we've already agreed to. Whether we handle it as representatives of our neighborhood, doing the watching or doing that work, or whether we hold an outsider accountable for coming in and causing some conflict. But that we, instead of sending them to the jail and the criminal justice system, we can sit them down and say, 'Look, this is how you've affected our community'.

I think that's a lot more powerful for people than having to spend the night in jail, because that's not accountability. Accountability is looking into people's faces who you have possibly violated and to answer to them directly.

sc: Which brings us to Restorative Justice. Are people familiar with that term?

Basically it's the idea that the victims of a crime, the perpetrators, and members of a community come together to deal with the issue at hand by all taking active roles in the process. It can involve restitution or accountability that doesn't involve jailing somebody or imprisoning somebody. Restorative justice also opens spaces for people to come together and mitigate conflicts, or undo 'wrongs' done to someone or a group. Restorative Justice can even question what is crime, what is right or wrong, as well as taking into account what the motives behind a crime that might need to be addressed, like drug addiction or miscommunication.

Restorative Justice has a long history in this country. It's also sometimes called Reparative justice. The state and its entities have absorbed some of it, as far as community restitution is in the form of community service. Where someone can do something 'good' with their time like volunteering at a nonprofit for committing a so-called crime, instead of jail. That's sort of their bastardization of it. But we're talking about real Restorative Justice, where we really take people out of the criminal justice system and try to question what justice means.

Another quick topic is the idea of decriminalization under current legal systems. Decriminalization is not the same as legalization. Decriminalization reduces the severity and punishment of so-called offenses—sometimes even removing the illegal status all together. This can be for any numbers of things that are considered criminal on the law books these days, like drugs. Marijuana is an example. In many states it's being decriminalized where people don't have to go to prison or jail for it anymore. The difference in decriminalization and legalization is that decriminalizing allows more organic and dynamic reversal of draconian laws that can be interpreted differently to fit the needs of particular communities. Whereas legalization sets up a whole new set of archaic regulations and bureaucracy that is supposed to be good for everyone without much interpretation. Again, using marijuana as an example, in decriminalized states people can grow their own for medical use in a variety of ways, mostly independent businesses; but in legalized states it all has to adhere to certain rules of the way it's grown, which end up favoring big business and lawyers.

We need decriminalization now! Especially for non-violent offenses. Let everybody out of the prisons now! Because we have over three million people in prisons and supervised release now, through county, city, state, and federal. Let's get them out of the prison for drugs. It's all bullshit.

The continued criminalization is more than just largely black and brown communities and drugs, but immigrants also. We need sanctuary cities. We need places that are safe for people to be, because the economic systems of capitalism have destroyed their communities and people come here wanting to have better lives; they shouldn't be criminalized for it.

I don't believe in borders at all, because they're artificial and they uphold corporations and the state. But we need safe places for people to be that are immigrants to this country. It's not a crime to want a better life.

DR: A lot of people think we are a sanctuary city in Austin. We are far from it. We have a small resolution that makes a nod towards that, but we are one of the highest counties in the country that are turning misdemeanor accused criminals over to ICE (Immigration Crime Enforcement), and have the highest deportation rates in the country for misdemeanor offenses. We're supposed to be this liberal bastion in Texas, but we're actually exporting more people accused of misdemeanor charges than Houston or Dallas, with much larger immigrant populations.

Remember, if you call the police on an undocumented person,

there are severe risks to them. You might be sending them off to another country. They can't get back, they can't make money, they can't support their families. This isn't just 'get them out of my face, they're bothering me'. So remember again what the risks are for your privilege; that you are a citizen (if you are), and remember not everybody has those same privileges as you do.

sc: Let's not forget the corporate vampires. If you pay taxes, you're paying for all this criminalization. You're paying for new prisons to be built, that all these companies—GEO Group, Corrections Corporation of America—that make a lot of money jailing immigrants and prisoners. Think about that. Private prisons turn a profit on incarceration. Of course they want to fill the prisons.

The only prisons that we need are for elected officials! If we're going to have them at all.

Audience: Yes!

sc: When we're taking back control, that means that we all will have to do the dirty work too. We all have to take out the garbage at some time. We can't just rely on these giant bureaucracies and institutions. It's about taking direct action, taking control of our lives individually as communities instead of waiting on others. Part of that is learning to deal with conflict and being accountable to each other. We need to set up conflict mediation places in every community for everybody to participate in, and learn to get along with people, even when we disagree. And I disagree with a lot of people!

The other thing in the social safety net that would help is the decriminalization of homeless people, like we talked about earlier. But people are homeless a lot of time not because they don't have access to housing or food, but really because they have drug and alcohol issues, criminal records, they can't get a job, and lack a good education. There's myriad issues.

It's always easy to call the cops and make it all go away. Just punching buttons on a phone. It's harder, but not impossible, for us to work together to create localized social safety nets and communities. Again, not the big giant bureaucratic institutions that are everywhere, all over the place, but in each of our local neighborhoods, so that people can have access to them right then.

DR: Right. There's an example here in Austin. We have a needle exchange program. It's a truck and it's at certain places at certain times, and gives out clean needles to reduce the incidence of HIV and hepatitis infections amongst drug needle users. It's actually been criminalized in Texas for a long time. We're the last state where it's a criminal activity. People came together years ago who saw a need and said 'we can save some lives' are still doing it despite the laws. In addition to access, they provide resources and services to support people in getting off drugs or medical complications. That's direct action. That's taking the harder path.

These are things we can do that really won't engulf your life. But you can support these projects and ideas like these. You can help build them. And that's all it takes sometimes to really save people from these institutions.

Thank you for coming out!

sc: Thanks everyone! It's important that we are coming together to talk about these issues because that's how we're going to build power from below. It's going to take all of us to challenge the systems of oppression that dominate right now. There's more of us than there are of them, and I think we have to remember that.

Afterword:

By Lara Messersmith-Glavin

Let's try something.

I want you to close your eyes and say out loud the names of the people who have really inspired you to make this world a better place. If you're on the bus right now, whisper them. If you're in a library, just think them to yourself, or mutter softly so you can feel the shape of the sounds on your lips. What are their names?

Some of you will jump straight to the heavy hitters: W.E.B. DuBois. Murray Bookchin. Emma Goldman. Alice Walker. Karl Marx. John Trudell. Judith Butler. Ursula Le Guin. Malcolm X. Others will recall the artists who first lit you up inside, who put sound, voice or image to frustrations or longings you didn't know you'd had: Crass. Karen Finley. Marjane Satrapi. Public Enemy. Frida Kahlo. Joan Baez. Ministry. Ai Weiwei. Jello Biafra. Banksy. Mia Zapata. Others will remember friends, family, mentors—the people who showed you it was OK to care: Your kid brother. Your first serious crush. Your seventh grade science teacher. Your drug counselor. Your mom.

Let the list grow. Watch your own mental evolution scroll out before you as you follow those names forward in time or back. Watch them connect like a web to the choices you have made in your life, for better and worse; see how they link to the things you've read, the things you've seen, the jobs you've held, the troubles you've borne. Notice how you have carried them with you, how they, in turn, have carried you—through the doubt, through the ups and downs, through the work you take on and the disappointments you face.

Now think about the way they made you *feel*. How many of

them lit you up like a paper lantern, turned you from your heavy, clay despair or resignation to something lighter, something capable of flight and flame? How many of them made you feel powerful? How many made you feel like other worlds were possible? How many of them were *positive*?

Most? All?

Now, ask yourself: how many inspired you by filling you with shame, by telling you that you were doing things wrong, by insisting that there was one path and one path only, regardless of the destination? How many made you feel like shit?

I hope none.

As we work to develop critiques of the structures and patterns that exist, as we identify oppression in ourselves as well as in the systems around us, we sometimes mistake the symptom for the sickness. We see ourselves playing out the negative scripts we've learned, repeating the abuse, the patriarchy, the racism—and we blame the person more than the problem. Our critical habit can turn in on itself; we get lost in finding what is wrong in one another, and we forget how to inspire and to heal. This is the key: if we want to transform this world into something that is a clear reflection of our dreams, our love, our highest ideals—or even just a place where everyone has an equal chance to thrive—then we need more folks talking about what we *can* do, about what we hope for.

As I read through the pages of this book, I am struck by a number of things: one, how accessible these ideas are, and how clear things feel when stated simply. We don't need a state. We need to support one another. Solidarity is a real thing, a force—solidarity is an action. Sometimes it's good to be reminded that the way things are is neither necessary nor inevitable. We can't make these changes alone, and every small shift is a victory. With every action, every thought, we either recreate or challenge the status quo. Change is accomplished by work, and by the work of everyone, together.

So what does the work look like? It looks like walking the talk. It looks like listening to others. It looks like finding allies in unexpected places, and being willing to meet people where they're at. It means being willing to get dirty, and knowing that, while the ideas can be clear, the process never is, and the outcome is never quite what we expect.

In every interaction I've ever had with scott crow, I've been reminded of his unflagging kindness, his active appreciation, his ability to talk with nearly anyone. He reminds me that this is what helps people stay committed to struggle, to dream beyond the simple answers and to have the courage to try new ways of doing things, to risk failure in the hopes of finding a better way. It's the commitment to the ideas that I value, and the willingness to follow that faith and see the results of those actions in daily life: Feeding each other. Protecting one another. Talking to each other. Listening. Celebrating even small victories and revolutions in thought.

This book is a great reminder of what we need. You won't find a prescription for correctness here, or a deep critique of others' work. What you will find are gentle examples of attempts to have an effect, to form relationships across ideologies and identities, and to stay close to the source of our inspiration.

We do it by doing it. Keep working. Together.

Emergency Heart Sutra

By John P. Clark
2013

For the Emergency Heart
The practice of Perfect Wisdom is nothing
But the practice of Perfect Compassion
For all suffering beings.
All things are nothing to it
Except as they alleviate
Needless ills and misfortunes
For all suffering beings.
Nothing it can do, say, or think
Matters apart from this.
Nothing it can gain or lose
Matters apart from this.
The Emergency Heart is distracted by nothing
Even its own distractions.
The Emergency Heart fears nothing
Even its own fears.
It goes beyond everything
To practice Perfect Wisdom that is nothing
But the practice of Perfect Compassion.
Gone, gone, gone fully beyond!
Beyond poor charity to Perfect Solidarity!
Emergency Heart Sutra!

FURTHER AND RECOMMENDED READING:

This is a selection of writings and films that have informed or inspired me, or in which I have participated. Many titles have come out in multiple editions over the years. In some cases, I have made reference to the latest version available.

ACTIVISM ORGANIZING, STRATEGIES, TACTICS:

BOOKS:
Nomad, Tom. *The Master's Tools: Warfare and Insurgent Possibilities* Berkeley: Repartee/Little Black Cart 2013

SITES:
Beyond the Choir: A great activism site for strategy and analysis on current tactics: https://beyondthechoir.org/

Organizing For Power: A site by Lisa Fithian that has good tools for grassroots political organizing: https://organizingforpower.org/

ALTERNATIVES TO POLICING:

BOOKS/ARTICLES:
Martín, José.'*Policing is a Dirty Job, But Nobody's Gotta Do It: 6 Ideas for a Cop-Free World*'. Rollingstone.com in 2013
http://www.rollingstone.com/politics/news/policing-is-a-dirty-job-but-nobodys-gotta-do-it-6-ideas-for-a-cop-free-world-20141216#ixzz3XUGbUBEq

Williams, Kristian, *Fire the Cops*. Montreal: Kersplebedeb, 2014

Williams, Kristian, *Our Enemies in Blue*. Oakland: AK Press 2015 2nd ed.

SITES:

Rose City Copwatch: Alternatives to Police:
https://rosecitycopwatch.wordpress.com/alternatives-to-police/

US Prison Culture Blog: Good source of links to alternatives:
http://www.usprisonculture.com/blog/2014/12/29/thinking-through-the-end-of-police/

ANARCHISM:

BOOKS/ARTICLES:
Ackelsberg, Martha. *Free Women of Spain: Anarchism and the Struggle for Women's Emancipation*. Oakland: AK Press, 1991.

Avrich, Paul. *Anarchist Voices: An Oral History of Anarchism in America*. Princeton, N.J.: Princeton University Press, 1995.

Bookchin, Murray. *The Spanish Anarchists: The Heroic Years 1868–1936*. New York: Harper & Row, 1978.

Bray, Mark *Translating Anarchy: The Anarchism of Occupy Wall Street*. London: Zero Books 2013.

Clark, John. *The Impossible Community: Realizing Communitarian Anarchism*. Bloomsbury, 2013.

Cornell, Andrew. *Oppose and Propose!* Baltimore: AK Press, 2011.

Curious George Brigade, *Anarchy in the Age of Dinosaurs*. Wisconsin: Yellow Jack Distro, 2003

Ervin, Lorenzo Komboa. *Anarchism and the Black Revolution*. Philadelphia: Monkeywrench Press, 1994.

Guerin, Daniel. *Anarchism*. New York: Monthly Press Review, 1970.

Gelderloos, Peter. *Anarchy Works*. Berkeley: Ardent Press, 2010.

Milstein, Cindy. *Anarchism and Its Aspirations*. Oakland: AK Press, 2010.

Pellow, David Naguib. *Total Liberation: The Power and Promise of Animal Rights and the Radical Earth Movement*. St. Paul: University of Minnesota Press, 2014

P.M. *Bolo Bolo* (30th Anniversary edition). Brooklyn: Autonomedia/Ardent, 2011.

Rosemont, Penelope. *Dreams and Everyday Life*. Chicago: Charles H. Kerr, 2008.

Shwarz, Sagris and Void Network, ed. *We Are An Image From the Future: The Greek Revolt of December 2008*. Oakland: AK Press, 2010.

Sitrin, Marina. *Horizontalism: Voices of Popular Power in Argentina*. Oakland: AK Press, 2006.

Tiqqun. *Theory of Bloom*. Berkley: Little Black Cart, 2012.

Tiqqun. *Introduction to Civil War*. Los Angeles: semiotext(e), 2010.

Ward, Colin. *Anarchy in Action*. London: Freedom Press, 1996

SITES:

Infoshop.org: https://news.infoshop.org

Anarchist News: https:// anarchistnews.org

Anarchist Library: https://theanarchistlibrary.org

Center For a Stateless Society: https://c4ss.org/

Libcom: https:// Libcom.org

Anarchy101: https://anarchy101.org

Anarkismo: https:// anarkismo.net

ANIMAL LIBERATION:

BOOKS/ARTICLES:
Adams, Carol. *The Sexual Politics of Meat: A Feminist-Vegetarian Critical Theory.* London: Continuum, 1990.

Hawthorne, Mark. *Bleating Hearts: The Hidden World of Animal Suffering.* Changemaker Books 2013

Singer, Peter. *Animal Liberation: A New Ethics for Our Treatment of Animals.* London:HarperCollins, 1975.

SITES:
TALON Conspiracy: An excellent repository of the radical animal liberation and environmental movements histories: http://thetalonconspiracy.com/

Black Panther Party:

Books/Articles:

Arend, Orissa. *Showdown in Desire: The Black Panthers Take a Stand in New Orleans*. Fayetteville: University of Arkansas Press, 2009.

Jones, Charles E.,ed. *The Black Panther Party (Reconsidered)*. Baltimore: Black Classic Press, 1998.

King, Robert Hillary. *From the Bottom of the Heap: The Autobiography of Black Panther Robert Hillary King*. Oakland: PM Press, 2009.

Shakur, Assata. *Assata: An Autobiography*. Westport, Conn.: Lawrence Hill & Co., 2001.

Films:

crow, scott and Ann Harkness. *Angola 3: Black Panthers and the Louisiana State Penitentiary*. PM Press 2008.

Common Ground Collective/Relief:

Books/Articles:

crow, scott. *Black Flags and Windmills: Hope, Anarchy and the Common Ground Collective*. Oakland: PM Press 2014 2nd ed.

Ilel, Neille. "A Healthy Dose of Anarchy." *Reason Magazine*, December 2006:
http://reason.com/archives/2006/12/11/a-healthy-dose-of-anarchy.

Nembhard, Jessica Gordon and Ajowa Nzinga. "African American Economic Solidarity." GEO Newsletter. #71, 2006.
http://www.geo.coop/archives/GEO71DS-AfricanAmericanEconomicSolidarity.htm

Solnit, Rebecca. *A Paradise Built in Hell: The Extraordinary Communities that Arise in Disasters*. New York: Viking, 2009.

South End Press Collective, eds. *What Lies Beneath: Katrina, Race, and the State of the Nation*. Cambridge: South End Press, 2007.

FILMS:
Imarisha, Walidah. *Finding Common Ground*. Third World Newsreel, 2006.

Holms, Rasmus. *Welcome to New Orleans*. 2005.

Flux Rostrum/Common Ground Collective. *Solidarity Not Charity*. http://tiny.cc/8nyabx.

SITES:
CG Stories: A resource and archive on the history and stories of the Common Ground Collective: https://cgstories.org/

MEDIA:

BOOKS/ARTICLES:
Canning, Doyle and Reinsborough, Patrick. *Re:Imagining Change: How to Use Story-based Strategy to Win Campaigns, Build Movements, and Change the World* Oakland: PM Press 2011

crow, scott. '*Like a tidal wave: a case for Agency*'. Agency Nov. 2014. http://www.anarchistagency.com/commentary/like-a-tidal-wave-a-case-for-agency/

Herman, Edward and Noam Chomsky. *Manufacturing Consent: The Political Economy of the Mass Media*. New York: Pantheon Books, 1988.

Radical Environmental:

Books:

Ongerth, Steve. *Redwood Uprising: From One Big Union to Earth First! and the Bombing of Judi Bari*. Self Published 2012
http://www.judibari.info/book

Bari, Judi. *Timber Wars*. Common Courage Press, 1994.

Best, Steven and Nocella, Anthony J. *Igniting A Revolution: Voices in Defense of the Earth*. AK Press, 2006.

Surveillance:

Books/Articles:

crow, scott. *Paper Tigers: Memoir of a Target under the War on Terror.* Oakland: PM Press 2016

Glick, Brian. War at Home: *Covert Action Against U.S. Activists and What We Can Do about It*. Boston: South End Press 1999.

Potter, Will. *Green is the New Red: An Insider's Account of a Social Movement Under Siege*. San Francisco: City Lights Publisher, 2011.

Williams, Kristian and Lara Messersmith-Glavin, and Munger, Will, eds. *Life During Wartime: Resisting Counterinsurgency*. Oakland AK Press 2012

Williams, Kristian. *Witness To Betrayal/ Profiles of Provocateurs*. Emergency Hearts/AK Press 2015.

Mother Jones Magazine 'Terrorists for the FBI' Oct. 2011 issue. Whole issue covers the topic: http://www.motherjones.com/special-reports/2011/08/fbi-terrorist-informants

FILMS:
Galloway, Katie and Kelly Duane De la Vega. *Better This World*. PBS, 2012.

Meltzer, Jamie. *Informant*. Music Box films, 2013.

WORKER COOPERATIVES:

BOOKS:
Curl, John. *For All the People: Uncovering the Hidden History of Cooperation, Cooperative Movements and Communalism in America*. Oakland: PM Press 2009

Dolgoff, Sam. *The Anarchist Collectives: Workers' Self-Management in the Spanish Revolution, 1936–39*. New York: Free Life Editions, 1974.

Krimerman, Len and Lindfield, Frank. *When Workers Decide: Workplace Democracy Take Root in North America*. Philadelphia New Society Publishers 1992.

Morrison, Roy. *We Build The Road As We Travel: Mondragon, A Cooperative Social System*. Philadelphia New Society Publishers 1991

ZAPATISMO AND ZAPATISTAS:

BOOKS/ARTICLES:
Eloriaga, Javier. "An Analysis of Evolving Zapatismo." *In Motion*, January 1997: http://www.inmotionmagazine.com/chiapas1.html.

Khasnabish, Alex. "Globalizing Hope: The Resonance of Zapatismo and the Political Imagination(s) of Transnational Activism." 2004. http://www.humanities.mcmaster.ca/~global/wps/Khasnabish.pdf

Marcos (Subcomandante) and Juana Ponce de Leon, eds. *Our Word is Our Weapon: Selected Writings.* New York: Seven Stories Press, 2001.

Links to the original interviews can be found here:

NOTE: *These are in alphabetical order, not order of appearance in book.*

A Conversation in Three Acts
Originally appeared: Firedog Lake; February 2014
http://www.scottcrow.org/a-conversation-in-three-acts-with-scott-crow/

Anarchy and Personal Transformation
Originally appeared: Paradigms Radio; January 2014
http://www.digitalpodcast.com/items/25654727

Anarchist Story-Telling: Reflections on News Media as a Site of Struggle
Interviewed conducted as part of M. Tedrow's doctoral thesis and for future book.

Black Flags and Windmills: Autonomy and Liberation After Disaster
Originally appeared: STIR magazine; April 2012
http://stirtoaction.com/scott-crow-interview/

Brick by Brick
Originally appeared: *Earth First! Journal* Vol. 34 No. 2 - Beltane/Spring 2014
http://earthfirstjournal.org/newswire/2014/06/26/beltane-2014-feature-brick-by-brick-an-interview-with-scott-crow/

Counter Narratives: on Anarchism, Pragmatic Ethics, and Going Beyond Vegan Consumerism
Originally appeared: Animal Voices Radio; 2014
http://animalvoices.ca/2014/07/29/counter-narratives-scott-crow-on-anarchism-pragmatic-ethics-and-going-beyond-vegan-consumerism/

How I Learned To Not Care About Winning Over Cops To Join Occupy Wall Street
Originally appeared: Diebenow.org; September 28, 2011
    http://www.diebenow.com/content/exclusive-interview-scott-crow-or-how-i-learned-not-care-about-winning-over-cops-join-occupy

The Liberatory Potential of Worker Co-ops: A Look at Ecology Action and Treasure City Thrift
Originally appeared: The Cooperative Oral History Project; January 2012
    http://coophistories.wordpress.com/scott-crow/

Shifting Culture Without Government
Originally appeared: Medium; February 2013
    https://medium.com/american-dreamers/b0b346416485

Social Movements and State Repression
Originally appeared: Z Magazine; December 2010
    http://zcomm.org/zmagazine/social-movements-and-state-repression-by-darwin-bondgraham/

The Unheard Story of Hurricane Katrina: Blackwater, White Militias & Community Empowerment
Originally appeared: Media Roots / Breaking the Set TV; Sept. 2014
    http://www.mediaroots.org/hurricane-katrina-unheard-blackwater-white-militias-community-empowerment/

When It's Broken: On Accountability and Alternatives to the Police
Presentation at: Peaceful Streets: Police Accountability Summit Austin, TX; July 2012
    https://www.youtube.com/watch?v=-M9iskkyX3I

Acknowledgements:

I am extremely grateful to the following on this project:

Tom Nomad for his editorial hand guiding this whole process and helpful feedback.

Lara Messersmith-Glavin for writing a wonderful afterword, and her inspiring story telling.

RA Washington and GTK Press for being so inspiring in their projects and giving me a space to air some evolving ideas in print that might have been lost in the internet databits.

My collaborator **Tony Shephard** on another excellent book cover!

Elaine J. Cohen for great editorial feedback, collaborations, conversations, and friendship.

Shelley Fleming at Wordranch for transcriptions and edits.

Leon Alesi for the photo and having fun at shows.

Ryan Walker for the interior book design.

John P. Clark for the poem, exploration of ideas and friendship.

Deb Russell for being a great co-organizer and collaborator.

My love **Ann** for, among others things, giving me support and space to put ideas down.

And to all the journalists who took the time to engage in conversations over the years and allowed GTK to use their work for this project: **Darwin BondGraham, Nathan Diebenow, Jonny Gordon-Farleigh, Anne Gessler, Grayson, Abby Martin, Vic Mucciarone, Kit O'Connell, DJ Pangburn, Matt Tedrow, Baruch Zeichner.**

Shout outs and love:

Stella Alesi, Ashanti Alston, Aragorn Bang!, Theresa Baker-Pickering, Kilaika Anayejali Kwa Baruti, Belinda Bonnen, Tyson Breuax, Derrick Broze, Nate Buckley, Javier Sethness Castro, James Clark, Jake Conroy, Chris Crass, Brian D. Ryan DC, Jenny Esquivel and Petey of Sacramento Prisoner Support, Adrián Flores and Lindsey Shilleh of El Rebozo Cooperativa, Lauren Gazzola, Chris Hannah and Jord Samolesky of Propagandhi, Josh Harper, Mark Hawthorn, Jen Justice Harney, Sole AKA Tim Holland & Yasamin Holland, Ramsey Kanaan, Gabriel Kuhn, Justin Kay, Amy Love, Shannen Maas, Daniel McGowen and Andrew of NY Anarchist Black Cross, Paul and Silas Messersmith- Glavin, lauren Orenalas, Scott Parkin, Kelley W. Patterson, Leslie James Pickering, Susana Pimento, Lauren Regan, Penelope Rosemont, Josie Shapiro, Lauren Regan, Alexander Reid Ross, Ryan Shapiro, Amanda Schemkes Daphne Silverman, Dave Strano, Connor Stevens, Chris Steele AKA Time, Kevin van Meter, Kristian Williams, Jeff Wirth, and the ever lovely Mariann Wizard.

Agency, Anarchist Black Cross, AK Press, Angola 3 Support Committee, Breakdancing Ronald Reagan, Bunny Alliance, Burning Hearts media, Carpe Locus Collective, Center For a Stateless Society, CrimethInc, Earth First! Journal, Fifth Estate, Jericho Movement, Little Black Cart, Monkeywrench Books, No New Animal Labs!, P& L Printing, PM Press, Ragblog, SHAC 2.0, Treasure City Thrift, Whichside Podcast, Zapatistas

Anyone whose hosted me, organized events, fed me food or drinks or brought me to colleges over the years THANK YOU! Lastly to all the individuals, collectives and groups engaged in liberation on their terms.

scott crow Reader Bios:

scott crow is a speaker, story teller, author and organizer proudly from a working class background. He has spent his varied life as a musician, coop business co-owner, political organizer and 'green collar' worker. The FBI spied on him for a decade as an alleged domestic terrorist threat for political activities without charges being brought. He is the author of *Black Flags and Windmills: Hope, Anarchy and the Common Ground Collective* (PM Press) and the *forthcoming books Setting Sights: Histories, Praxis and Reflections on Community Armed Self-Reliance* (PM Press), *Paper Tigers: Memoir of a Target under the War on Terror* (AK Press) and *Standing on the Edge: Towards A Politics of Possibilities* (PM Press). He contributed to the books *Grabbing Back: Essays Against the Global Land Grab* (AK Press), *Witness To Betrayal* (Emergency Hearts/ AK Press), *Black Bloc Papers* (LBC) and *What Lies Beneath: Katrina, Race, and the State of the Nation* (South End Press). He lives in Austin, Texas.
He can be found online: https://scottcrow.org

Lara Messersmith-Glavin is a writer/storyteller, editor, organizer, and educator. She is a member of the editorial collective of the journal Perspectives on Anarchist Theory, and serves on the board of the Institute for Anarchist Studies. She lives and works in Portland, Oregon, alongside her partner and son.
Find her at: https://queenofpirates.net, https://anarchiststudies.org

John P. Clark lives in New Orleans where his family has been for twelve generations, He taught philosophy and environmental studies at Loyola University and has long been active in international movements for ecology, social justice, and grassroots democracy. His books include *Max Stirner's Egoism, The Anarchist Moment, Anarchy, Geography, Modernity: Selected Writings of Elisée Reclus,* and *The Impossible Community: Realizing Communitarian Anarchism*. His alter ego Max Cafard wrote *The Surregionalist Manifesto and Other Writings*, *FLOOD BOOK*, and *Surregional Explorations*. An archive of over two hundred of his articles and papers can be found at http://loyno.academia.edu/JohnClark. He is a member of the Education Workers Union of the IWW.

Tom Nomad is the author of *The Masters' Tools*, the editor of Dialogues Press and journal, and a member of the Institute for the Study of Insurgent Warfare. He is currently working with Guide to Kulchur, a worker owned printshop and bookstore in Cleveland.

Guide To Kulchur is a bookstore and cooperative project founded by Lyz Bly, Ph.D. and RA Washington and acts as an incubator for emerging and marginalized voices within the print medium. Our projects include Cleveland Books 2 Prisoners, GTK Press, The Cleveland Zine Archive, The Sally Tatnall Black Box, and The Cooperative Print Workshop.

GTK PRESS:
PUBLISHER: RA Washington
CREATIVE JOURNAL EDITOR: Krystal Sierra
CREATIVE JOURNAL ASSOCIATE EDITOR: Zena Smith
DIALOGUES JOURNAL/NON FICTION EDITOR: Tom Nomad
DIALOGUES JOURNAL/NON FICTION ASSOCIATE EDITOR: Andy Cameron
GRAPHIC DESIGN: Ryan Walker
COOPERATIVE PRINT WORKSHOP: Gus Hurst, Avalon Hurst

GUIDE TO KULCHUR: Text, Art & News consists of:

Renée Hurst
Andy Cameron
Avalon Hurst
Tara Bess Balsam
Richard Schulte
David Egbert
François Fissi Bissi OkraKongo
Evan Gloosekap
Dan McCarthy

Krystal Sierra
Tom Nomad
Ryan Walker
Gus Hurst
RA Washington
Justine Strehle
Lizzard Nekokitty Freeman
Christina Keegan

guidetokulchurcleveland.com